WELCOME BACK

MICHAEL

A COMMEMORATIVE EDITION

This is an unauthorized biography of Michael Jordan.

PUBLICATIONS INTERNATIONAL, LTD.

Photo credits:

Front cover: **Otto Greule/Allsport USA.**

Allsport USA: Al Bello, Jonathan Daniel, Stephen Dunn, Otto Greule, Jim Gund, Scott Halleran, Ken Levine; **John Barrett/Globe Photos, Inc.; Edie Baskin/Onyx; Duomo:** Dan Helms, Mitchell Layton, Rick Rickman, William R. Sallaz, Ben Van Hook; **Nathaniel S. Butler/NBA Photos/Sports Illustrated Picture Service; Brian Drake/MGA/Photri, Inc.; Focus On Sports; Gamma Liaison:** Jon Levy, Michael Springer; **Sam Griffith Studios; David Liam Kyle; NBA Photos:** Andrew D. Bernstein, Nathaniel S. Butler, Lou Capozzola; **Outline Press**: Craig Blankenhorn, Neal Preston; **Retna:** Steve Granitz; Susan Sherry; **Sports Illustrated Picture Service:** John Biever, Nathaniel S. Butler, Walter Iooss, Jr., David Klutho, Richard Mackson, John W. McDonough, Manny Millan, Buck Miller, Patrick Murphey-Racey, Time, Inc., Tony Tomsic, David Walberg; **Carl Sissac; Sportschrome.**

Pages 6-61 written by: **Bob Sakamoto**

Bob Sakamoto has been a sportswriter for more than a decade with the *Chicago Tribune,* where he spent four years covering Michael Jordan and the Chicago Bulls. Sakamoto received his master's degree in journalism from Northwestern University and began his career as a feature writer with the *Chicago Daily News.* His articles have appeared in numerous publications, including *Bulls Eye, Chicago Sports Profiles,* and *Hoops NBA Yearbook.*

This is an unauthorized biography of Michael Jordan.

Louis Weber, C.E.O.
Publications International, Ltd.
7373 North Cicero Avenue
Lincolnwood, Illinois 60646

Permission is never granted for commercial purposes.

Manufactured in U.S.A.

8 7 6 5 4 3 2 1

ISBN 0-7853-1009-6

CONTENTS

WELCOME BACK MICHAEL

Above: **Michael Jordan has touched the lives of so many, not just with his athletic prowess, but with his honest, genuine love of people.** ***Opposite:*** **Michael blew the world of basketball wide open with his exploits and gave birth to the term "hang time."**

It was one of those rare special surprises, like getting a bonus from your boss or flowers from your sweetheart. Michael Jordan, said those in the know, may be, could be, coming back to basketball.

The rumor in March 1995 sent shock waves throughout the country. Nike stock shot up. Production in Illinois workplaces was on the rise as fans were rejuvenated by MJ's possible return. A priest in Chicago referred to the second weekend in Lent as "Michael Jordan Weekend."

When His Airness announced on March 18, 1995, that he would indeed dribble again—releasing a statement that said simply, "I'm back"—Chicagoans threw their hands to the heavens while NBA execs slapped high-fives.

What drove Michael away from baseball and back to basketball? Many theories have been bandied about: Jordan grew weary of bush-league bus rides. He no longer wanted to be mixed up in the baseball strike. And, of course, he missed the spotlight.

Jordan said he hungered for basketball while he was playing pickup games down in the minor leagues.

"Each time I played, my appetite was whetted," he said. "I missed the games, the teammates, the atmosphere."

This book pays tribute to Air Jordan. It recounts his rise to the throne, the championship years, and his year-and-a-half hiatus. The book is a way of saying . . . Welcome back, Michael. It's good to have you home again.

PREPARING FOR TAKEOFF

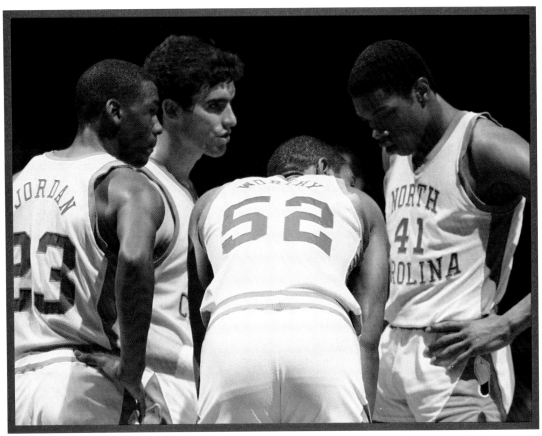

Above: **A young Michael Jordan** *(left)* **with Tar Heel teammate—and later NBA rival—James Worthy** *(center).* ***Opposite:*** **Michael at home with his parents.**

It all began on February 17, 1963, when Michael Jordan was born in a Brooklyn, New York, hospital. While his early life wasn't always smooth sailing, he was surrounded by a loving, caring family. It's this love of family that is at the heart of Michael Jordan.

Watch Michael carefully, listen to his words. There is the unmistakable presence of an inner discipline. Someone taught him early on the virtues of courtesy, honesty, and respect for elders. Nothing is more important to Michael than his family. "My family has been my inspiration to succeed," Michael said. "My childhood means a lot to me. They were pushing me and fighting with me and helping me become the man I am today. My personality and my laughter come from my father. My business and serious side come from my mother."

Michael's late father, James, was able to impart to his son a respect for humble beginnings and a feeling of being grateful for what you have. Listen closely to the words of the father, and remember when you hear them from the son.

"It's not really what color you are," his father once said, "it's who you are. It's not what you amass or have that makes you different, it's your personality. You can have the most money in the world and still be a jerk. You can have no money at all and be the nicest man in the

world. People who like you for what you are, those are your real friends. We made sure [the kids] understood that lesson."

"That's the greatest lesson I've learned from my parents," Michael said. "I never see you for the color. I see you for the person you are. I know I'm recognized as being black, but I don't look at you as black or white, just as a person. I think one of the reasons I've been accepted by people of so many different races is that my personality fits that."

Growing up in Wilmington, North Carolina, Michael was closest to his older brother by a year, Larry. The ferocity of their backyard one-on-one games has taken on near-legendary proportions. For the longest time, Larry was a better player, usually getting the best of his little brother in these sibling showdowns. "Oh yeah, I used to be able to take him most of the time," said Larry, who competed for one season in the World Basketball League for players 6'4" and under, dunking two-handed, backwards, with ease. "But once he began shooting up and getting taller, I had more trouble staying with him."

"Those backyard games really helped me become the player I am today in a lot of ways," Michael said. "Larry would never give me any slack, never took it easy on me. He'd rather beat me up than have me beat him in a game. I learned a lot about being competitive from him."

Actually, basketball wasn't Michael's first love. If he had a choice, he would have been the next Ernie Banks or Hank Aaron. Baseball was his best sport growing up, particularly when he was merely a normal-sized youngster. "My favorite childhood memory, my greatest accomplishment was when I got the Most Valuable Player Award when my Babe Ruth League

team won the state baseball championship," he said. "That was the first big thing I accomplished in my life, and you always remember the first."

Michael Jordan, however, wasn't born a basketball phenom. He wasn't some hardwood child prodigy like Isiah Thomas, who was competing with 13-year-olds when he was seven. Perhaps his late blossoming contributes to the modesty and humility he displays today. He became serious about the sport as a sophomore at Laney High School, averaging 25 points a game as the star of the junior varsity. He expected a promotion that season to the big time where he would become the next darling of North Carolina.

It never happened. Instead, he was cut from the varsity squad and had to resign himself to junior varsity competition. He worked on his game that summer in relentless fashion to make certain he never again suffered such a fate. Over and over he practiced moves that would one day become part of his seemingly

limitless repertoire. Even his beloved baseball had to take a backseat to this determination to prove to the Laney coach and everyone else that a mistake had been made the previous season.

As a junior, Jordan not only made Lynch's club, but Michael worked his way into the starting lineup by averaging 20 points a game. "He could do more things than the average high school player," recalled Ruby Sutton, Laney's volleyball and boy's tennis coach. "Still, he was a normal student. Because he was good at what he did, that didn't make him a conceited person. And yes, he stuck his tongue out even back then."

Jordan's game began to come together as a senior, as he averaged 23 points a game. Although he was named to the Mid-Eastern All-Conference Team and the McDonald's All-America Team, college recruiters weren't exactly staking out the Jordan home trying to sign him to a national letter of

Opposite: **Glimpses of future greatness. MJ soars for North Carolina with the trademark tongue extended.** ***This page:*** **Just one jewel in Michael's crown was the opportunity to show his stuff in the '84 Olympics. Team USA took home the Gold.**

intent. Teachers and administrators at Laney even urged him to enroll at a service academy or at least set his sights realistically—like attending a small Division III college where he would get a chance to play. He decided to attend college in North Carolina and play for the Tar Heels.

There are any number of glorious moments in the tradition-steeped basketball legacy of the University of North Carolina. If you ask any Tar Heel fan or probably most college basketball fans in the state for the most memorable event, though, they'll tell you all about the NCAA championship game in 1982 when a freshman stepped up and hit the game-winning shot.

The Michael Jordan we know today was already beginning to emerge. Yet, even though that first-year Tar Heel was Michael Jordan, we're still talking about some kid who had just turned 19 years old making a shot that had immense ramifications on the entire North Carolina program.

That shot, played again and again each year at March Madness, came in the final game of the tournament against Georgetown. The score was 62-61 Hoyas, with 31 seconds left on the clock. Michael gets the ball for one of the most famous shots in the history of the game. He is 16 feet away from the basket on the left wing and there are just 15 seconds showing on the clock. Up he goes, unleashing that patented Jordan jumper. Bam! He hits it, and the Tar Heels prevail 63-62.

Jordan was good enough to be named the Atlantic Coast Conference's Freshman of the Year, no small accomplishment in what often is considered the best college basketball league in the land. He went on a European tour that summer, his first basketball experience abroad. He returned to Chapel Hill and began dominating the game.

Jordan went on to average 20 points, grab 5.5 rebounds, and shoot 53.5 percent in his second season, averaging close to two

steals a game. He averaged 19.6 points a game his junior season, good enough to lead the ACC, with 5.3 rebounds a game while shooting 55.1 percent. His career high in college was 39 points against Georgia Tech as a sophomore. During his final year at Chapel Hill, before skipping his senior season for the pros, Jordan played on a Carolina team that was considered the best college team in the country. It was a huge disappointment when the Tar Heels lost to Indiana 72-68 in the "Sweet 16" of the NCAA tournament. Early foul trouble for Jordan and Sam Perkins forced coach Dean Smith to pull them out, giving the young Hoosiers a chance to build confidence and believe they could upset a team that had been ranked No. 1 for most of the season. That final Jordan club finished 28-3, including a 14-0 mark in the competitive ACC.

Nevertheless, *The Sporting News*'s college Player of the Year didn't come to the NBA on a down note. Michael wound up playing for the U.S. on the Olympic basketball team at the 1984 Summer Games in Los Angeles. The coach of that team was none other than the Hoosiers' Bobby Knight, the man who had sent Jordan home a loser in his college finale.

MJ's father once said, "I've got to believe one thing. One day, God was sitting around and decided to make himself the perfect basketball player. He gave him a little hardship early in life to make him appreciate what he would earn in the end, and called him Michael Jordan."

YOUNG BULL

Above: In 1984, a change was brewing in the City of Big Shoulders. Unbeknownst to most of the world, an explosion called Michael Jordan was waiting to happen. *Opposite:* A human fireworks display.

In the 1984 draft, the Bulls wound up with Michael. Selecting first, the Houston Rockets grabbed Akeem Olajuwon. Next came the Portland Trail Blazers, and they opted for center Sam Bowie. The Bulls were "forced" to take Jordan.

Michael came to town highly recommended, yet nobody expected him to be the biggest superstar in the sport. The home opener in Chicago Stadium even made it appear that the $6 million, seven-year contract might have been a bit too much. In his NBA debut, a visibly nervous Jordan made just five of 16 shots for 16 points in a 109-93 victory over Washington.

After scoring 21 points in a loss at Milwaukee, Jordan cut loose in his third game with 37 points in beating the Bucks at home. Jordan led the way to a 116-110 win by scoring 20 of his team's final 26 points. Milwaukee guard Mike Dunleavy, later a coach for the Lakers and Bucks, said, "He showed tremendous poise. Very few rookies can come into the NBA and dominate like this kid." These were the days when the Bulls were known as "Michael and the Jordanaires." Orlando Woolridge might have been the only other legitimate player.

Those who attended Michael's debut at the L.A. Memorial Sports Arena saw a move that only Jordan could have pulled off. First, he hit a

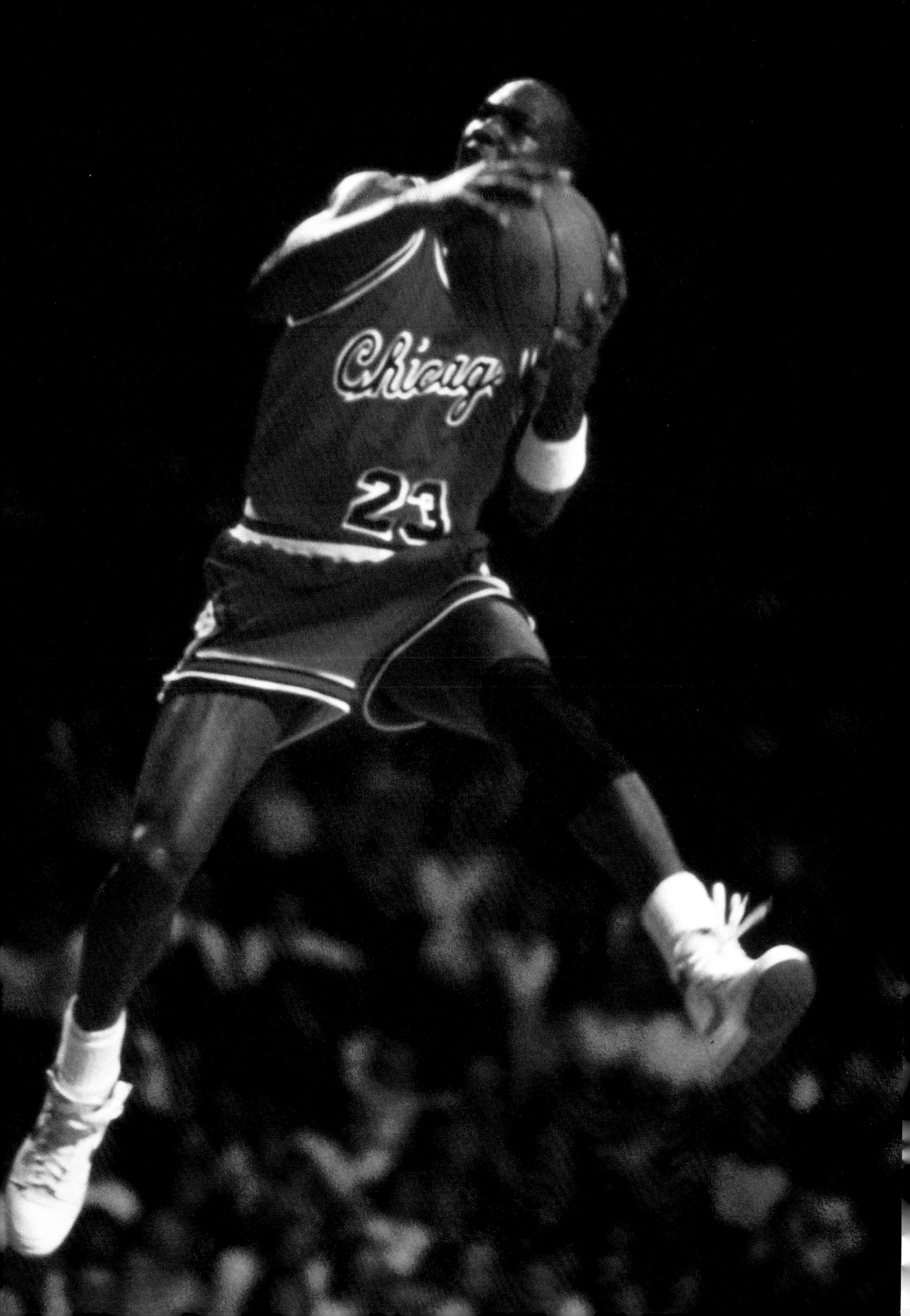
Chicago
23

jumper to tie the Clippers at 100. With 1:26 left, he smothered Norm Nixon defensively and forced the Clipper star to shoot an air ball. Caldwell Jones grabbed the miss and unleashed a two-handed pass.

Jordan caught up with the ball somewhere beyond midcourt and began loading up for one of his patented dunks. Derek Smith caught Jordan from behind and wrapped him up in a bear hug as Jordan was in midair. Somehow, with amazing grace, Jordan was able to get off a shot while crash-landing, unable even to see the basket. Two points, foul, free throw good. Bulls win.

Jordan wound up being named Rookie of the Year by averaging more than 28 points a game, and being among the league leaders in steals.

Jordan's second season was one of tumult that culminated in the single greatest individual postseason performance in NBA history. It all started when Jordan fractured a

bone in his foot in the third game of the season at Golden State, costing him 64 games. The Bulls wanted to play it safe, letting him sit out the remainder of the season.

The competitive Jordan wanted no part of it. Sticking to his rehabilitation schedule religiously, he thought he could still lead the team to a playoff berth. Jordan continued his onslaught until owner Jerry Reinsdorf finally agreed that Jordan would play, but only in small incre-

---

When Michael Jordan became the first NBA player in 24 years to crack the 3,000-point barrier, it was accomplished with the kind of flair and drama that Wilt Chamberlain could never have hoped to match.

---

ments. After Jordan started playing like the Michael of old, Reinsdorf finally rescinded the time limit. Unchained, Jordan led the Bulls into the playoffs. He was fresh compared to the tired athletes who had just completed an 82-game grind. Bulls coach Stan Albeck thought he had a chance to sneak up on the Celtics.

There was no way the Bulls could match up with Boston's Larry Bird, Kevin McHale, Robert Parish, and Danny Ainge. Albeck instead called for the Bulls to transform the game into a two-on-two contest, Jordan and Woolridge against the two best Celtics.

It almost worked. In game one of the best-of-five series, Jordan rocked and rolled through Boston Garden for 49 points in a 123-104 loss. He had 30 points by halftime, the polite applause of fierce Boston partisans, and the Celtics more than a little worried.

That proved to be just a preview for game two. It would be a day

Opposite, left: **The 1984 Rookie of the Year gives a flying lesson.** *Opposite, right:* **Rock and Roll!! Mike scored a playoff-record 63 points in this double-overtime loss to Boston.** *This page:* **Number 23 became the first player in 24 years to crack the 3,000-point barrier.**

basketball fans will never forget. There was a look on Jordan's face Sunday that said he would not be denied this time. If he had to beat the Celtics one-on-five, so be it. Michael almost did. Jordan scored a playoff-record 63 points in a 135-131 double-overtime loss that pitted the game's best individual talent against the best team.

Jordan hit off-balance shots and regularly took three and four Celtics to the hoop. In one memorable sequence, he dribbled between his legs and then around Bird, blew by Dennis Johnson, took off over McHale, and double-pumped a layup with Parish flailing away helplessly. One against four and Jordan wins. The Celtics, however, went on to sweep the series.

What those fortunate enough to have tickets witnessed in 1986-87 is probably the most electrifying, crowd-pleasing individual season in the history of the game. When Michael Jordan became the first NBA player in 24 years to crack the 3,000-point barrier, it was accomplished with the kind of flair and drama that Wilt Chamberlain could never have hoped to match.

When a 6'6" guard scores 3,041 points, everyone takes notice. Michael's 1986-87 average of 37.1 points a game led the league, beginning a run of seven consecutive scoring titles (from 1986-87 through the 1992-93 season). He accomplished it in the face of double- and triple-teaming defenses combined with other "anti-Air" strategies.

This season was the year Jordan would forge an identity that would be fire-branded into the psyches of opposing coaches and players who tried to contain him. All the great games and outrageously terrific moves Jordan had made before would be eclipsed during this season. When he scored the 63 points in the playoff loss to Boston the year before, it was foreshadowing—

ominous to those who played against him, joyful for those who wore the Bulls' colors.

Michael began to stretch the limits of credibility, as he put on a scoring exhibition that delighted fans everywhere. On one Friday night in February, he bombarded the New Jersey Nets for 58 points,

13

breaking by two points the Bulls' regular-season record for points in a game held by Chet Walker since 1972. In dropping 26 of 27 free throws, Michael shattered the club mark of 25 held by Artis Gilmore. Jordan had 34 points by halftime, finishing with 11 in the third quarter and 13 in the fourth as the Bulls ran away from the Nets 128-113.

Twice, Jordan reached the 61-point mark, once against the Detroit Pistons and once against the Atlanta Hawks, which culminated a sensational three-game stretch. The final week of the season began with Michael burning the Pacers for 53 points, eight assists, and four steals in a 116-95 win on April 12. He hit 14 of his first 18 shots in a performance that left the guys from Indiana shell-shocked.

The very next night, he went off for 50 points, nine rebounds, four steals, and three blocked shots in a 114-107 win over the Bucks in Milwaukee. He completed this tri-

fecta of Michael-mania three nights later with a 61-point, 10-rebound, and four-steal performance in a 117-114 loss to the Hawks. The 61 points tied the regular-season club record he had set earlier against the Pistons.

Only one other NBA player, Chamberlain, had scored 50 or more points in three consecutive games. Jordan's outburst against Atlanta elevated him into the rarified air of the 3,000-point club. He also scored an NBA-record 23 points in a row.

Moreover, Jordan scored 50 or more points for the eighth time that season. Most NBA players never score 50 in their careers. All-time greats Elgin Baylor and Rick Barry, a pair of prolific scorers, scored 50 points 17 and 14 times, respectively, in their careers.

The public fell in love with Michael, a love affair that grew more passionate with every game. Kids and grownups sensed a certain

humility about him, that he didn't feel he was any better than the next man and, personality-wise at least, could fit right in with the common folks.

Jordan was sitting in an airport terminal one afternoon that season, awaiting a commercial flight with his teammates. This was during spring vacation and hundreds of school kids were making their way to various destinations. All it took was one of them to spot Jordan and, before long, hundreds had mobbed him seeking an autograph or just wanting to reach out and shake his hand. Watching this, a flight atten-

Top, left: **Perpetually swamped with requests for autographs, Mike always tried to please his adoring public.** *Top, right:* **A rare talent takes a moment to reflect on his first three years.**

> **"[Jordan] is absolutely a young man totally at ease with destiny. He is comfortable with his role as a superstar."**
> **—60 Minutes *producer Bill Brown***

player to share his winnings with his teammates," said Clyde Drexler, who also competed. "He's a classy guy. I wish he was on my team. I've never heard of a basketball player doing this. It's good to see a guy with a kind heart." Bulls teammate Gene Banks said, "He's a genuine individual, one in a million. He's one of God's special children."

"I'm very happy with my season," Jordan said. "I'm surprised I scored

this many points, and I don't think I'll ever have another season like this offensively."

As he walked out of the Stadium locker room for the final time in that memorable season after the Celtics had swept the Bulls 3-0 in the playoffs, Jordan glanced back and said: "You know, maybe this will be the greatest season I ever have."

dant offered Jordan the sanctuary of a private office until the plane was ready to take off. "No, that's okay," Jordan replied. "I'll just stay here and sign these autographs. The way I look at it, this is just a small thing I can give back to a game that has given me so much."

During this season, Jordan began rubbing elbows with the biggest celebrities. *60 Minutes* interviewed him, filming a segment with Jordan and correspondent Diane Sawyer playing a game of one-on-one before the interview. "I wondered, 'Is there anything wrong with him?'" *60 Minutes* producer Bill Brown said. "The answer is, nothing. [Jordan] is absolutely a young man totally at ease with destiny. He is comfortable with his role as a superstar. He is also very alert to the possibilities of the pressures on him. He is totally comfortable with his role in life. Even if his celebrity went away, he would be comfortable with himself. The extraordinary athletic prowess, the sudden fame, an instant millionaire, and yet, here is this kid still unaffected."

This was also the season he graced the cover of *GQ* magazine and outpolled Magic Johnson as the No. 1 vote-getter in the fans' All-Star balloting. Michael won his first NBA Slam-Dunk Contest, dividing the $12,500 prize money among his teammates. "It's very rare for a

*O*ne of the most amazing moves in Michael's career took place during his 63-point assault against Boston in the 1986 NBA playoffs. It began with MJ going one-on-one with Larry Bird while other Celtics looked on in case Bird needed help. Jordan dribbled between his legs and flew past Bird with that lightning first step. At the same time, he zipped around Celtic Dennis Johnson. Continuing on his quest, Michael took off past Kevin McHale and then double-pumped a lay-up over Robert Parish. Jordan's 63 points were an NBA playoff record.

JORDAN VS. THE BAD BOYS

Above: Michael's success forced the Pistons to invent new methods with which to defend him; these became known as "The Jordan Rules." *Opposite:* Bill Laimbeer of Detroit can't stop a patented Jordan drive.

After the 1987-88 campaign, a panel of select nationwide media finally came to their collective senses and gave Michael Jordan his due. No. 23 finally became No. 1. Jordan was finally voted the NBA's Most Valuable Player, an honor many thought overdue.

Jordan was untouchable in his fourth season. In a league full of thoroughbreds, he was Secretariat. He became the first player in NBA history to win the scoring title (35 points a game) and be named

Defensive Player of the Year in the same season. That was just the beginning. He led the league in steals (3.16 a game), blocked more shots than 16 starting centers, was first-team All-NBA and All-Defense, was the league's slam-dunk champion, and became the only player ever to block 100 shots and record 200 steals in consecutive seasons. He also reached four NBA and eight club playoff records and became the first player to score 50 points in consecutive playoff games.

For the first three weeks of the season, Jordan & Co. were the hottest team in pro basketball. Their 4-0 start was the best in the Bulls' 22-year history. At 9-2, they had the NBA's best record. They went to 12-3, and made the Celtics and the Lakers begin to wonder if they would have to make room at the top.

In the opener before 18,688 fans at Chicago Stadium, Jordan poured in 36 points, and the Bulls whipped the 76ers 104-94. After the opening game came a staunch road test in Atlanta. Jordan issued a pregame

challenge to the Hawks, saying it was about time the Bulls realized they were good enough to beat Dominique Wilkins's gang on its own turf. Jordan's comments found their way into an Atlanta newspaper, and the talented Hawks were riled. No matter, Jordan had 29 points, seven assists, and six steals in a 105-95 win.

Back home, the Bulls routed the Nets 103-85, the fourth-straight time they'd held an opponent under 100. Jordan had a workmanlike 36 points, seven rebounds, and six steals. The Indiana Pacers came to town and the high-flying Bulls may have overlooked this lowly bunch. Charles Oakley committed a critical turnover late in the game allowing Chuck Person to hit the winning

basket in a 111-110 loss before 18,676 disappointed Bulls fans.

The Bulls went to 6-1. Despite an early home loss to the Pistons that would foreshadow things to come, the Bulls continued to roll. They upset the Celtics 107-102 in Hartford, Connecticut, and followed with a 103-101 win in Milwaukee to give them an NBA-best 5-0 mark on the road.

Coming off that prolific scoring spree the year before, Jordan kept things low-key until erupting for 47 points, nine assists, three steals, and three blocks in a rousing 105-101 win at Utah. Early in the third quarter, Jordan drove and dunked easily over 6'2" Jazz guard John Stockton. "Hey Jordan, why don't you pick on somebody your own size," shouted

This page, left: **Michael's magical one-hand shot frustrates the Pistons.** *Above:* **Jordan goes to the boards with mate Dave Corzine.** *Opposite, above:* **Cleveland's Craig Ehlo realizes that "you can't touch this" when it's Jordan time!** *Opposite, below:* **Jordan wows the crowd.**

a Jazz courtside season ticketholder who loved to razz opposing teams. Jordan glanced over at him, making a mental note as he raced back upcourt. On the very next play, Jordan again came slashing towards the basket, this time slamming it over 7', 290-pound Melvin Turpin. As he ran upcourt, Jordan looked right at the Jazz fan and asked, "Is he big enough?" The fan shook his head and laughed and Jordan smiled.

Jordan was named the NBA's Player of the Month as the Bulls won 12 of their first 15 games. The Bulls would eventually level off, but not No 23. In a 111-100 victory over the Cleveland Cavaliers December 17 at the Stadium, Jordan racked up 52 points on 20-of-31 shooting, including 30 points in the second half. It was more fore-shadowing of what MJ later would do to the Cavs in the playoffs. Said Craig Ehlo, who was defending Jordan: "I was handed my breakfast, lunch, and dinner all in one night."

In a raucous Stadium rumble on January 16, Jordan had 36 points, 10 rebounds, and 10 assists in a 115-99 win over the Pistons. During the game, a pair of 6'9" musclemen, Oakley and Rick Mahorn, squared off in a violent fight. Coach Doug Collins, who didn't always see eye-to-eye with Oakley, jumped into the fray and put a headlock around Mahorn. Incensed, Mahorn grabbed the Bulls coach and threw him over the scor-er's table, where Bulls TV analyst Johnny "Red" Kerr caught him. Undaunted, Collins launched him-self back at Mahorn and was slugged in the face. By the time order was restored, a bruised Mahorn and a battered Oakley were ejected.

With the All-Star Game in Chicago, Jordan put on a critically acclaimed show for the home folks and a national TV audience. First,

he successfully defended his slam-dunk title over runner-up Dominique Wilkins, relying on a free-throw line jam choreographed by Julius Erving and a "Kiss the Rim" slam that garnered a perfect score. The next day, he scored 40 points in leading the East to victory and was awarded the MVP trophy. More foreshadowing.

Jordan began revving up for a record-breaking playoff scoring binge in the final two months of the regular season. He had 52 points in a loss to Portland and 50 in the Bulls' first Stadium win over the Celtics since December 17, 1985. After that game, Kevin McHale observed: "Jordan singlehandedly dismembered and dismantled all of us." On March 23, after scoring just 16 points in the first half and bristling from a Collins comment

that "David Wingate is kicking your butt," Jordan scored 33 second-half points to Wingate's zero in a 118-102 win over Philly.

Then, in perhaps his best game of the regular season, Michael put up 59 points, hitting 20 of his first 24 shots, in a 112-110 win over the Pistons in the Silverdome. With 24 seconds left, Jordan blocked a shot by Isiah Thomas, and with four seconds to go, he hit the winning free throws. This may have provided the motivation for the Pistons to eventually devise a defensive strategy later to be called "The Jordan Rules." It would come into play when the two teams met in the second round of the playoffs.

Not long after, Jordan reached agreement with the Bulls on a new eight-year contract that would pay him $28 million. No wonder he

was so charged up down the stretch. He had 47 points in a win over the Knicks, and in the season finale he scored 46 points in a clutch win over the Celtics. It gave Chicago the third-best record in the East, as Jordan clinched his second-consecutive scoring title.

Jordan had a career playoff series in leading the Bulls past Cleveland 3-2. He had 50 points in the opener, a 104-93 win in which he equaled or set six club records. In game two, MJ went off for 55 points in a 106-101 win. He was the first guy ever to do the 50-50 thing in successive postseason games. In between, he shot a 75 at a Chicago area golf course. At that point, he had broken or tied two NBA playoff records and 14 club marks.

Jordan had "only" 38 points and nine assists in the game three loss and was held to 44 when the Cavaliers evened the series. He had 39 and Scottie Pippen a playoff-high 24 in the decisive win back home. Jordan finished the series averaging an absurd 45.2 points a game when scoring was supposed to drop below regular-season standards. It was a record for a five-game series.

Pistons assistant coach Ron Rothstein is credited with designing "The Jordan Rules," 13 defensive sets to counter Jordan's favorite and most effective moves. It worked in the opener of the 1988 Eastern Conference semifinals as Jordan was limited to 29 points in a 93-82 Detroit win. Bulls guard Sam Vincent foiled the strategy in game two with 31 points as the Bulls won 105-95 and went home with the best-of-seven series even.

In game three, Detroit was the epitome of its Bad Boy image. Just 1:37 into the game, Bill Laimbeer set an illegal screen into Jordan and was whistled for a foul. Jordan claimed that, after the whistle, Laimbeer intentionally elbowed him. Incensed, Jordan took a swing at an opposing player for the first time in his career, missing with a right hook. A melee erupted, emotions flared, and the Bulls were never the same. Accustomed to such guerilla warfare, the Pistons swept both games in Chicago, 101-79 and 96-77. Jordan scored only 24 points in game three and 23 two days later. The Bulls were eliminated back in Pontiac, Michigan, 102-95, as Jordan had 25 points, eight rebounds, and eight assists. Still, something about him impressed Pistons coach Chuck Daly.

"He's Superman," Daly told the *Chicago Tribune*. "I don't know how he does it, where he gets that energy, his intelligence, his instinct for the game. It's like Philadelphia when Julius Erving was there. I'm

A MICHAEL JORDAN MOMENT

*O*n April 3, 1988, Jordan scored 59 points at the Pontiac Silverdome to single-handedly defeat the Bad Boy Pistons. Besides hitting 20 of his first 24 shots, Michael also blocked a shot by Isiah Thomas with 24 seconds left. Then, with just four ticks to go, No. 23 converted the winning free throws for a 112-110 victory. This provided the motivation for Detroit to devise its Jordan Rules, 13 different defensive sets designed to control Michael's offensive moves.

telling the people of Chicago: 'You're seeing something there that only comes around once in a lifetime.'"

Michael raising his level of play, and that of his teammates, to championship caliber was many years in the making. The 1988-89 and 1989-90 seasons, though, were frustrating for Michael, the Bulls as a team, and the city of Chicago. The Bulls came so close to the Finals both seasons. And the despised Detroit Pistons came away with the trophies both years.

Opposite, left: Jordan isn't afraid to go head-to-head with the league's big men. Here he mixes it up with the Knicks' Patrick Ewing. **Opposite, right:** Michael's explosive drive to the basket paralyzes an army of Cavaliers during the '89 playoffs. The Great One's amazing series helped the Bulls defeat Cleveland in five games.

Left: **Despite Michael's patented fadeaway jumper, the Pistons twice stopped Chicago in the Eastern Conference finals.** *Opposite:* **MJ and Detroit's Isiah Thomas, two of the NBA's best guards, share a spirited rivalry.**

guard in a Collins experiment, Jordan had a stretch where he recorded seven consecutive triple-doubles, an unheard-of achievement. He finished the season with 15 triple-doubles, including 12 in the final 24 games.

In October 1988, the Bulls weren't considered one of the top five teams in the circuits. It took a miraculous Jordan jumper to propel them to that level. Few basketball players get the opportunity to hit a dramatic, game-winning shot that has so much impact it will go down in history, yet Michael has been twice-blessed. First came the game-winner that gave North Carolina the NCAA championship over Georgetown in 1982. Then, seven years later, after the 1988-89 season, Jordan hit a difficult shot that began the deterioration of a one-time NBA title contender.

The tape of his last-second shot that eliminated the Cleveland Cavaliers from the 1989 playoffs has been replayed countless times. With six seconds left in the game and Cleveland trailing by a point, Cavs coach Lenny Wilkens unveiled a piece of brilliant strategy. He had Ehlo inbound the ball. None of the Bulls paid much attention to Ehlo—with stars Mark Price, Larry Nance, and Ron Harper the likely big-shot choices. Craig snuck past the Bulls defense, took a return pass, and scored a layup.

There were three seconds left when the Bulls inbounded the ball from halfcourt with 20,000 Cavaliers fans in Richfield Coliseum screaming for the home team to hold on for just three ticks of the

Coming off the high of their 50-win season of 1987-88, the Bulls fell off a bit the following year, finishing 47-35, fifth best in the Eastern Conference. Jordan won his third-consecutive league scoring title, averaging 32.5 points a game. He was third in the NBA in steals and 10th in assists. He was awarded the Schick Pivotal Player of the Year honor and *The Sporting News* named him Player of the Year. He

scored 52 points three times in November, burning the Celtics, 76ers, and Nuggets. In Denver, he broke his own club record by scoring 30 points in the fourth quarter. He had an NBA- and season-high 53 points in a loss to Phoenix in January and four days later scored 33 points against the 76ers to reach the 10,000-point milestone faster than any other player except Wilt Chamberlain. Switched to point

clock. Everybody in the building and, indeed, across America watching this national telecast knew where the ball was going. Bulls assistant coach John Bach had long ago nicknamed this the "Archangel Offense." Said Bach: "That's where we put the ball in his hands and say, 'Save us, Michael.'"

Jordan broke to the ball with Nance and Ehlo in hot pursuit. Ehlo was Jordan's defender and Nance simply abandoned his assignment, as he was so intent on stopping Jordan. Michael got the ball, pivoted, took a dribble past Nance, and from the right of the free-throw line took off. Jordan pumped once as his body drifted horizontally to the left, freeing himself from Ehlo, who appeared to give Jordan a little nudge. Still gliding to his left, Jordan shot the ball at the basket. It was the same sensation as hitting a moving target. Somehow, Jordan swished the 15-footer for a 101-100 victory. He landed on both feet, leaped into the air, and waved his fist. Michael was mobbed by his ecstatic teammates. The Richfield Coliseum turned into a gigantic mausoleum as 20,000 stunned partisans sat in silence, not wanting to believe what they had just witnessed.

"There's nothing like it in the world, that feeling of having the ball in the final seconds as the

clock slowly ticks off, going up and hanging in the air and then hitting the shot," Jordan said. "Man, that is total control. There's just no other feeling like it, none."

In the next round of the playoffs, the Bulls went on to defeat the New York Knicks 4-2. Despite pulling a groin muscle, Jordan averaged 35.6 points and 9.6 rebounds in the six games. In the opener, he registered his first playoff triple-double with 34 points, 12 assists, and 10 rebounds.

**"There's nothing like it in the world, that feeling of having the ball in the final seconds as the clock slowly ticks off, going up and hanging in the air and then hitting the shot."
—Michael Jordan**

The Bulls had finally made it to the Eastern finals, but again they fell short against the Pistons, losing in six games. For the postseason, Jordan averaged 34.8 points, eight assists, and seven rebounds as he began demonstrating to critics he

was more than simply a scorer. He did replace Bob Love as the club's all-time leading playoff scorer.

Jordan reached another milestone during the 1989-90 season when he torched Cleveland for a career-high 69 points in a 117-113 overtime win at the Richfield Coliseum. The 1989-90 season was Michael's sixth, and his fifth full season, discounting his sophomore year when he missed 64 games with a broken foot. Jordan supplanted Love as the Bulls' all-time leading scorer, as he won his fourth-consecutive scoring title, averaging 33.6 points a game. He also led the NBA in steals with 2.77 a game. Expanding his game, he averaged 6.9 rebounds and 6.3 assists a game while leading the Bulls to a 55-27 record, their best in 18 years. They wound up with the second-best record in the East, behind only arch-rival Detroit.

The Bulls knocked off the Bucks 3-1 in the first round of the 1990 playoffs. Chicago then got by the troublesome 76ers 4-1, with Jordan scoring 49 points in game three at the Spectrum. Once again, it was the Motor City against the Second City in the Eastern Conference finals. This time, each team won its home games, with the Pistons squeaking by in the seven-game series with the final game at the Silverdome. This series did mark the first time Michael had beaten Detroit's anti-Jordan defensive system when he tallied 47 points in game three and 42 in game four, both wins at the Stadium.

This was the third consecutive year in which the Pistons had shut the door on Chicago. However, the Bulls were pounding harder and harder with each playoff effort. Would Jordan and his mates knock the door down? The answer would come in the spring of 1991, when they would meet again.

SWEET REVENGE

Above: Michael Jordan discusses a game-winning strategy with teammates during the 1991 NBA Finals. *Opposite:* Jordan soared past Patrick Ewing and the Knicks in three straight games to clinch the opening round of the playoffs.

The Bulls had the greatest regular-season success in franchise history during 1990-91, winning 61 games, the most in the Eastern Conference. Michael won his second MVP Award and his fifth-consecutive scoring crown with 31.5 points per game. He also averaged 6.0 rebounds and 5.5 assists a game, and totaled 223 steals. These numbers would be astounding for any other player in the league. By his seventh season, though, these stats seemed almost mundane for Michael Jordan.

"I just try to have the best season possible and be as consistent as possible," Michael said. "This year is a little more special because my teammates have really stepped up to give me the contribution I have needed and we have needed to put us in a position to win [the NBA Championship]."

To capture the NBA title, Chicago would have to win four series. The third stop would be against the Pistons, but first the Bulls would have to knock off New York.

From the opening tip in this first-round series with the Knicks, the Bulls proved they meant business. In game one, they slammed the Knicks 126-85. Chicago's tough interior defense held New York center Patrick Ewing to six lousy points. "I'm frustrated by the whole situation," said Ewing. "They whipped us. Beat us by 41."

New York came back in game two, dominating the boards and leading 65-61 in the fourth quarter. But the Bulls went on an 18-5 run and won 89-79. The series moved east for game three. The Knicks took a 12-point lead in the contest, but Jordan and reserve Will Perdue led the Bulls back. Michael poured in 33 and the Bulls walked off with a clinching 103-94 win.

Next stop? Philadelphia. Chicago's defense held its foe to under 100 points for the fourth game in a row, as the Bulls beat the Philadelphia 76ers 105-92 at Chicago Stadium. Sir Charles Barkley scored 34 for the Sixers, but he couldn't do it alone. Chicago's aggressive defense held Philly to 37-percent shooting. Jordan scored 29 points. Ditto in game two. Jordan again scored 29, Scottie Pippen added 23, and the Bulls thumped the Sixers 112-100. The Chicago big men dominated this game, outrebounding Philly a resounding 42-27.

The Bulls finally lost a playoff game in game three. Jordan scored 46 points (despite a bad knee), but the Sixers won the game 99-97. Hersey Hawkins's three-pointer with 10 seconds left won it for the home club. No such luck in game four, a contest played on Mother's Day. Jordan (25), Horace Grant (22), and Pippen (20) overwhelmed the Sixers, opening up a 21-point lead, and the Bulls presented their moms with a 101-85 victory.

The Bulls added an exclamation point in game five. Pippen couldn't miss, scoring 28 while Jordan was a monster on the boards. This 6'6" wonder scored 38 points and grabbed 19 rebounds. Michael averaged 33.4 points during the five games. "I thought we had a good shot," Philadelphia coach Jim Lynam said after the series was finished, "but Jordan took over." The

final: Chicago 100, Philadelphia 95. Bring on those Bad Boys.

For three years in a row, the Bulls had been ousted from the playoffs by the Pistons—that collection of sneering, whining, bullying Bad Boys. By 1991, Chicagoans were sick of the Pistons, and they wanted them bad.

When the Detroiters rolled into town, all they saw was red. Jordan got into the face of the Pistons, especially Joe Dumars and Dennis Rodman, proving to the Motor City Mad Men that the Bulls would not be intimidated.

In game one, Chicago outboarded the Pistons 43-26, while their starting front line outscored Detroit's 42-17. The Bulls won 94-83. Michael did not have a good game one, shooting six-for-15 for 22 points and turning the ball over six

times. "I didn't shoot the ball well today, and I basically had a bad game, at least offensively," Michael said. "You've got to give my supporting cast a lot of credit."

In game two, Jordan (33) and Pippen (21) came up big, while the Pistons squirmed in frustration. Again, the Pistons couldn't score inside, and the Bulls trotted off the Stadium floor with a 105-97 win.

For game three, the series moved to Detroit, but the story was the same. Chicago smoked the nets in the first quarter and then coasted the rest of the way. Chicago's front-line starters outscored Detroit's 56-12, while Jordan chipped in 33. The Bulls won the game 113-107 and now led three games to none.

"The demon isn't dead yet," said Grant, "but we can cut off its head Monday."

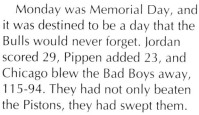

Monday was Memorial Day, and it was destined to be a day that the Bulls would never forget. Jordan scored 29, Pippen added 23, and Chicago blew the Bad Boys away, 115-94. They had not only beaten the Pistons, they had swept them.

Detroiters did not take this loss well. In games three and four,

Images of the '91 playoffs.
Opposite page: **Jordan drives past Philadelphia's Armon Gilliam during the Bulls' second-round win over the Sixers.** ***Above:*** **The NBA title is so close, Michael can almost taste it.** ***Above, right:*** **Soaring above Detroit's Mark Aguirre, Jordan wins a jump ball in the Eastern Conference Finals.** ***Right:*** **Looking to drive right, Mr. Intensity fixes his gaze on Joe Dumars. The Bulls swept out Dumars and the rest of the Pistons in four straight games.**

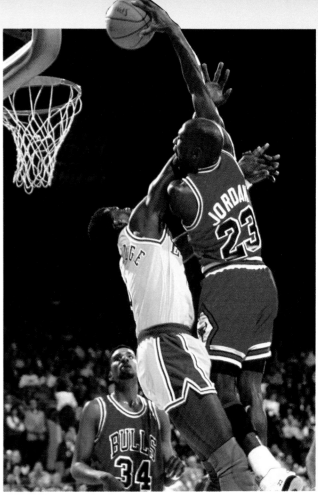

Pistons Aguirre and Rodman each drew technical fouls. In the finale, Rodman shoved Pippen hard, and then he threw a basketball into Jordan's stomach. With eight seconds to go in game four, the Pistons walked off the court, unwilling to congratulate the new champs.

"We're not used to this," said Dumars, "and it's a terrible feeling."

Dumars found little sympathy in the Windy City. Having handily managed the Pistons, all attention would now focus on the final series against Los Angeles.

The Lakers had defeated the Portland Trail Blazers for the Western Conference crown, and now they traveled to Chicago for the opening of the NBA Finals. L.A.'s Magic Johnson had won five

NBA titles, but now he would have to attempt to do it in the Bulls' den, Chicago Stadium, widely held as the loudest arena in the NBA. Chicago was coming off 15 consecutive playoff wins in front of the raucous home folks.

The series would center around two stars—Magic and Michael—and in game one, the two superstars did not disappoint. It was a tight, heart-thumping affair destined to go to the wire.

Johnson nailed two three-pointers at the end of the third quarter to put L.A. up 75-68, but then Chicago came back to score 10 in a row. The Bulls led 91-89 with 14 seconds left when L.A.'s Sam Perkins, Michael's old college teammate at North Carolina, canned a three-

> ## "We're not used to this, and it's a terrible feeling."
> —Joe Dumars, after the Bulls swept Detroit in the 1991 Eastern Conference finals

point shot. Jordan could not match the shot seconds later, when he missed on an 18-footer. The three-pointer provided the winning margin and the Lakers, looking like grizzled champions, won at Chicago Stadium 93-91.

Jordan scored 36 points with 12 rebounds and eight assists in game one, while Johnson recorded a triple-double.

The Bulls grabbed opportunity by the horns for game two and proceeded to blow the roof off the Stadium. The Bulls routed L.A. 107-86. Jordan, who scored 33 points, connected for 15-of-18 field goal attempts. At one point, he went up for a tomahawk jam, then changed his mind in mid-air and flipped in a left-handed layup.

"We were very nervous in the first game," Michael said. "I knew we'd be more relaxed tonight. We didn't do things differently; it was just that our energy level was higher." Scottie Pippen scored 20 points, but more importantly took over much of the defensive burden of guarding Magic and did a masterful job. On the other hand, Michael again proved his versatility by moving to low-post defense to guard Vlade Divac. Grant (20 points), Bill Cartwright (12), and John Paxson (16) came up big.

Regaining the momentum, Michael and the Bulls flew into Los Angeles looking to take it to the purple and yellow at the Great Western Forum. This contest would prove to be as exciting as game one. The Lakers opened up a 13-point lead in the third quarter, as Laker big men Perkins (25 points), Divac (24), and Worthy (19) beat the Bulls inside. But, in the fourth, Chicago rode on the backs of its big men—Pippen, Grant, and reserve

Opposite, left: **Clearly not awed by the Western Conference champion Lakers, Jordan fixed his gaze on the NBA crown.** *Opposite, right:* **Michael goes tongue-first over Orlando Woolridge to slam home a basket.** *This page, left:* **In the driver's seat, Michael steers past the Lakers in the Finals.** *Above:* **Despite double-teaming, Jordan had a great series. Here he splits the defense and shoots over Magic Johnson.**

Cliff Levingston—and the Bulls climbed their way back.

Divac converted on a three-point play to give L.A. a 92-90 lead with 11 seconds remaining, but Chicago wasn't through. Jordan canned a jumper to send the game into overtime. Michael heated up in O.T., sinking two reverse layups and canning another shot. The Bulls outscored the Lakers 12-4 in the extra frame and won the game 104-96.

Their backs to the wall, the Lakers were prepared to blast the Bulls in game four. It was Chicago, however, that lacquered L.A. with a suffocating defense, winning 97-82. Michael had 28 points and a career playoff-best 13 assists.

Magic scored 22 points and had 11 assists in the game and Divac had 27 points and 11 rebounds. The numbers tell the rest of Chicago's defensive story: Perkins one-for-15 for three points; Worthy six-for-16 for 12 points; Byron Scott four points; Terry Teagle six points; A.C. Green one-for-five for five points. "We've got a great opportunity to finish it now," Michael said. "But we know it's not going to be easy."

Jordan is a better player than prognosticator. Two Laker starters—Worthy and Scott—were injured and could not play in game five. When they tipped off, however, the replacements responded. Elden Campbell and Tony Smith sparked L.A., and by the end of the third quarter the score was tied.

The tension grew thick in the fourth. Magic hit Campbell for an alley-oop slam, and then Pippen followed with a three-point jumper. With the score tied 93-93, Paxson went to work. He nailed two jumpers, a layup, and two more jumpers. Chicago moved ahead 105-101. Pippen followed with two free throws, Michael sank one, and the Bulls raced off the court with a 108-101 victory.

"It means so much," Jordan said after the championship victory. "All the things I've gone through, all the things the city has gone through. It was a lot of hard work, and what you see is the emotions of all that hard work paying off. Not just for me, but for this team and this city. It was a seven-year struggle. It's the most proud day I've ever had."

Michael had 30 points and 10 assists in game five to finish the series averaging 31.2 points, 11.4 assists, 6.6 rebounds, and 2.8 steals per game. He said this about being named Finals MVP: "I could care less. The whole team is the MVP. The whole city is the MVP."

Outside of the game of basketball, life continued to go on. Michael Jordan, superstar or not, had to deal with personal events like everyone else. Even though he received the ring, Michael would not forget a tragedy that took place that season. For six years, he had entered into a close friendship with Mickey Gitlitz, the personable, fun-loving owner of the Multiplex Fitness Club in north suburban Deerfield, where the Bulls practiced. It was in November 1990 that Gitlitz died from a cancerous brain tumor that he had battled for nearly two years.

It was a painful reminder that as much as Michael Jordan would love

In 1991, the Bulls finally advanced past their hated rivals, the Pistons, on their way to dethroning the Motown Maulers as NBA champions. Not allowing Detroit's roughhouse tactics to rattle him, Michael led the Bulls in an unexpected sweep of the defending two-time champs. The middle two games in the series were classic Jordan. He scored 35 points at the Stadium in a 105-97 victory, and followed up on the Pistons' home turf with 33 points, leading the Bulls in a 113-107 triumph.

> "He's a fun-loving person, he smiles, he's outgoing, and he tries to do the best he can at whatever he does."
> —*Michael Jordan, describing himself*

for the world to be fun and games and carefree times, a place where laughter and joy are the music we dance to, it can't always be.

Michael wants everyone in the world to smile more than they frown, to rejoice more than they hurt. This is the compassionate, human side of Jordan, a young man who remains as caring and considerate today as he was back in Wilmington, North Carolina.

He was once asked to describe himself: "He's a fun-loving person, he smiles, he's outgoing, and he tries to do the best he can at whatever he does. He feels like he's a role model for kids, and I would say he's good-looking." With that, Jordan let loose a grin. "But that might be saying too much."

Celebration! *Above:* Michael enjoys the taste of victory. *Upper right:* MJ relaxes with Paxson, Cartwright, Pippen, and Grant after clinching the title. *Right:* The MVP of the Finals lets the reality of victory sink in while clutching the championship trophy.

THE REPEAT

Above: **Knowing what it would take to do the nearly impossible, Michael fires up the team.**
Opposite: **Scottie Pippen and Horace Grant rally around MJ as they prepare to take the league by storm.**

Indelibly etched in our memories, forever to be shown over and over on highlight film and videos, is a gesture Michael Jordan made that really does sum up the 1991-92 season. It happened in the first game of the NBA Finals between the Bulls and the Portland Trail Blazers just after Jordan had hit a record six three-point shots in the first half of the Bulls' victory. As he was "Cadillacing" back upcourt in that all-too-familiar easy gait, Jordan turned toward the TV cam-

eras and shrugged his shoulders, both hands uplifted as if to express: "What can I say?" It was the same feeling opposing coaches and players have felt ever since Michael entered the league. When Jordan's game is on, there is absolutely nothing that can be done to stop him short of a flagrant foul.

There is another scene that will go down in history. About half an hour after the Bulls had repeated as NBA champions, having already drenched one another in cham-

pagne and mugged for the TV cameras, Jordan led the players back onto the Stadium court for a curtain call. Very few of the nearly 19,000 fans had left the building. Celebratory music kept blaring out over the the arena's sound system and nobody wanted this moment to end. Perhaps it was because this was the very first NBA championship that had ever been won at the Stadium. The Bulls had captured their first title at the Forum in Inglewood, a suburb of Los

Angeles. This time, the party was at the Big House on West Madison, and it looked like it could last all night long.

When Jordan & Co. reappeared, a tremendous standing ovation washed down upon the players. This was like a baseball player stepping back out of the dugout and tipping his hat in acknowledgment of the fans' adulation. The players waved at the audience and exchanged high-fives, not entirely certain how to conduct themselves since this was a new experience for everyone, players and spectators alike.

Leave it to Mike to figure out a way to charge up this party. He hopped up on the scorer's table, clutched the NBA championship trophy close to him, and began dancing. Before long, all 12 Bulls were up on this makeshift stage trying to be like Mike. More ovations. Network television had terminated its telecast just before the impromptu conga line. So when local TV stations televised it live on their late-night newscasts, it lent a special feeling to this accomplishment.

It was special indeed, particularly for Jordan, who called this season the most trying of his career. This was the year his squeaky-clean image that he painstakingly and meticulously shaped over the first seven years of his NBA career was somewhat tarnished. There had recently been several events—the publishing of the book *Jordan Rules,* his absence during the team trip to the White House, and much ado about some debts he had incurred through wagering on private games of golf and poker—that had cast him in a negative light.

Jordan's seven-year honeymoon with the press ended abruptly as would-be Woodward & Bernsteins saw career-making opportunities in bringing down a genuine American

hero. This entire process brought a new perspective to the formerly all-too-trusting Jordan.

"I began to understand that society builds up certain individuals only to bring them down in the end," he said. "I don't know if people these days really want a hero, if they really want to believe somebody can be so far up there. I'm beginning to think people would rather have those role models like myself brought back down to their level. I suppose in some way, it makes them feel like an equal.

"I think people have gotten a more diverse picture of Michael Jordan, not just from the positive side, but some negative stuff and humanistic stuff as well," continued Michael. "So, it's taken a lot of the

pressure off. Hopefully, we'll all learn something from this year. I know I've learned. I know I've matured."

This was the season Jordan would win his third MVP Award, becoming only the seventh player in league history to win the award three or more times. That put him in the exclusive company of Kareem Abdul-Jabbar (six MVPs), Bill Russell (five), Wilt Chamberlain (four), and Magic Johnson, Larry Bird, and Moses Malone (three). He won his sixth consecutive scoring title with a 30.1 average, leaving him one behind Chamberlain. Jordan also averaged 6.4 rebounds and 6.1 assists—an indication that he could expand other areas of his game as his Bulls' supporting cast

Opposite: They danced in the streets when Michael & Co. brought down the Stadium—and the city of Chicago—with back-to-back championship wins. This page: There is no easy path to greatness. It was through hard work, and performing the impossible as routine, that Michael led his team to their second title. He was rewarded with his third MVP award—only the seventh player in history to win it three or more times.

step up, he stepped up for us, and that's what a leader is all about. He gives so much to the game of basketball."

Jordan continued to provide leadership that led the Bulls to a 14-game winning streak early in the season and a 13-game string of successes in midyear. It added up to a 67-15 record, the best in franchise history and among the best in NBA history. There was a March game at Orlando where Scott Williams, Cliff Levingston, Craig Hodges, and Grant were clowning around playing baseball with a basketball five minutes before tipoff. That's the kind of regular season it was. The Bulls were so much better than their competition, they sometimes didn't take the game seriously. The Bulls trailed the expansion team by eight points at halftime.

That ticked off Michael. "You could see it at halftime," John Paxson told the *Chicago Sun-Times*. "He didn't say much, but he obviously wasn't pleased. He had that glare when he came out in the second half. You could see he was ready to do something." Jordan proceeded to score 18 points, hand out five assists, and steal the ball four times in the third quarter to personally provide his team with an insurmountable 20-point lead.

Jordan's intensity overflowed one night in Salt Lake City when the

began shouldering its part of the scoring load.

Bulls coach Phil Jackson told the *Chicago Tribune*, "More than ever this year, he deserved the MVP Award because of what he's been able to do—take some points off his scoring and figure out how to help his team in different ways, some not even statistical, and become a bet-ter player overall than ever before. And still carry us when we have to have him. It's the most auspicious award that you can receive in this league, and to win it back-to-back has to be tremendously sweet for him."

"You really can't say enough about the guy," said teammate Horace Grant. "When it was time to

A MICHAEL JORDAN MOMENT

Opposite, top left: **Mike's commercial endorsements were taking off.** *Opposite, top right:* **Michael and Patrick Ewing square off before a bitterly fought series.** *Opposite, bottom:* **Feats like this wild drive around a Cleveland Cavalier demonstrate MJ's desire to bring it on home.**

Since he has driven down so many lanes, it was only appropriate that Michael be given a lane of his own that anyone could drive down. A seven-mile strip of Interstate 40, north of Michael's hometown of Wilmington, was dedicated to him. "This gives the state of North Carolina a chance to say 'thank you,'" said the state's transportation secretary, Thomas Harrelson. "It's a privilege to have anything named after you," Jordan said, "especially when you're still living."

Bulls lost a heartbreaking triple-overtime game to the Utah Jazz in which Jordan hit a three-pointer to force a second overtime and was ejected for bumping referee Tommie Wood after Wood called a foul on him in the last second of the third OT.

This was the season the Bulls would convincingly stomp out the Bad Boys threat from Detroit, beating them four out of five times in the regular season. For the first time in his career, Jordan began to reli-giously follow a weightlifting program. In the past, he was worried that pumping too much iron would affect the delicate hair-trigger on his jump shot. But he decided to strengthen himself after enduring the physical beatings administered by the Pistons in the previous two postseasons.Yet, even as the Bulls were eclipsing one physical team, another, the New York Knicks, were on the horizon. Instead of Bill Laimbeer and Isiah Thomas, it would be John Starks, Charles Oakley, and Anthony Mason doing the intimidating.

Jordan should've been tipped off as to what kind of a season this would be when he got an emotional phone call from Magic early in November. The news was shocking. Jordan was one of the first people Johnson called to reveal that he had tested positive for the HIV virus that causes AIDS. Jordan took the call on his car phone and remembers being so stunned that he had difficulty at times staying on the road.

"I asked him what I should do about it because I was really confused," Jordan said to the *Tribune*. "And he just said: 'Live on. I'm going to be as positive as I can and I want you to be as positive as you can be.' I told him I loved him.

"Like most people in America, I was shocked, devastated by it. Myself and all the other players in the league have looked up to him, and we still look up to him. What he did [hold a news conference] took a lot of courage. He seemed so calm. Frankly, I wasn't as calm as he was."

Immersing himself in basketball, Jordan led the charge to show the world that the first NBA championship wasn't a fluke. He knew winning two in a row would bring him alongside Magic and Bird. The playoff road began with a sweep of the Miami Heat as a torrid Jordan scored 46 points in the opener and 56 in the clincher.

Next came a bitterly fought series against the Bulls' new rivals—the

Knicks. New York shocked the Bulls by capturing the series opener at the Stadium, 94-89, as Starks, Xavier McDaniel, Greg Anthony, and the rest of this Thug Bunch mauled their way to victory. The Bulls rebounded to win the next two games with Jordan contributing 32 points, nine rebounds, and two dunks in the 94-86 game three victory. Game four went to the Knicks, but Jordan came to the rescue in the pivotal game five by scoring 13 of the Bulls' last 19 points and finishing with 37. The Knicks evened the series back in New York, forcing a dangerous game seven when anything can happen. The Bulls prevailed easily, 110-81, and it was on to Cleveland and the Eastern Conference finals.

After splitting the first four games, the Bulls once again claimed the pivotal game five showdown, paving the way for their 4-2 triumph. Jordan scored 16 points in the fourth quarter of the clincher to set the Bulls up for an NBA title showdown with the Portland Trail Blazers. Many fans around the country felt it might be within the Portland team's grasp to steal the championship title.

Jordan opened up the first game against the Blazers in spectacular

fashion, scoring 35 points in the first half. He even included six three-pointers in the Bulls' 122-89 victory. "I was amazed, but I really wasn't embarrassed by it," Jordan said afterward. I really felt like, 'Hey, what can I say, it's happening.' I'm glad it's happening to me at this particular time."

"It was an amazing performance because you don't expect a player to stay hot during a period of the game that's so critical," coach Jackson said. "It was just a storm."

"The guy was unconscious," Grant added. "Whenever you see a guy like that, he's in his own zone. We were just out there watching for a while. We tried to shake his hand so that hopefully some of that hot shooting could rub off on us."

Portland evened the series with an overtime win in game two, 115-104, despite 39 points and 10 assists from Jordan. The Bulls asserted themselves in game three with a 94-84 win, with Jordan chipping in 26 points and seven rebounds. Back came the Blazers with a 93-88 triumph in game four, led by Jerome Kersey and Clyde Drexler's 21 points apiece. Michael finished with 32 points and six assists.

Once again, the Bulls played like the champions they are in game five. Jordan racked up 46 points, an all-time playoff high against Portland, as the Bulls won 119-106. Jordan's 33 points and 26 from Scottie Pippen fueled a comeback victory for the Bulls in game six. They prevailed 97-93, setting off the Stadium celebration.

"I feel very joyous," Jordan told the *Tribune.* "I'm not going to cry, but it's an unbelievable feeling. It caps off a remarkable season for me personally and for our team. This has been my most difficult year, but at the same time, it's been my most educational and maturing one. I made some mistakes. I learned

Opposite: In the '92 Finals, Mike smoked the Blazers. All Clyde Drexler and the Portland team could do was stand in awe, watching as Mike dominated. *This page, above:* Back-to-back! MJ hoists the second title trophy. *This page, right:* Soaking up the rays at a celebration in Chicago's Grant Park, Michael joins the city in celebrating its second championship victory.

more about the importance of how I, as a role model, must be even more cautious about what I do and with whom I associate. I'm just so glad I was drafted by the Chicago Bulls. I don't think I would be here today with back-to-back championships if I wasn't a Bull. I love playing here. I love the fans and I wanted to show them how much I love them and how grateful I am to them. I hope I play here forever."

"It was beautiful," Magic said. "I don't think people understand or realize that when you talk about a Larry Bird or a Michael Jordan, you won't be getting these guys anymore. It's hard to come up with guys like Michael. Fans have got to realize, this is it. You've got to absorb all of it because when he's gone, there's not going to be any more Michael Jordans."

THE THREE-PEAT

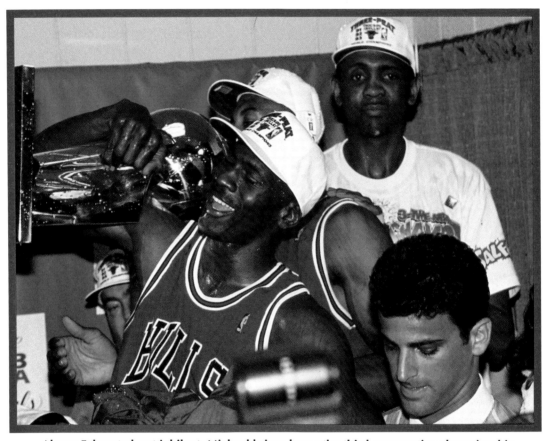

Above: **Exhausted, yet jubilant, Michael brings home the third consecutive championship trophy for Chicago.** *Opposite:* **Classic Jordan. Michael flies up and over the Knicks in the '93 Semifinals.**

The 1992-93 regular season brought Michael to another milestone. He scored his 20,000th point during a 120-95 victory over Milwaukee. In doing so, he became the second-fastest player to reach that plateau, accomplishing it in 620 games. Only Wilt Chamberlain was faster, racking up the 20 grand in just 499 games.

"It looks like I fell short of Wilt again, which is a privilege," Jordan said. "I won't evaluate this until I'm away from the game. I'm happy about it, but we still have a long season to go. I'm sure as I get older, I'll cherish it more."

The Bulls were nosed out for the best record and homecourt advantage in the East playoffs by the Knicks, but swept through the first two rounds with ease. With Jordan averaging 34.3 points, seven rebounds, and five assists, and shooting a torrid 6-of-13 from the three-point arc, the Bulls cruised past the Atlanta Hawks in three straight.

Cleveland was supposed to be a stern test, but the Bulls won four in a row with Jordan averaging 31 points, five rebounds, and five assists. Sir Michael put the finishing touch on the Cavs with another memorable shot in game four for the clincher.

That set up the confrontation everyone had anticipated, Bulls vs. Knicks. People were calling this the real NBA Finals, assuming the winner here would triumph over either Phoenix or Seattle in the West.

It was an emotional, bloody, hard-fought, gut-wrenching series, reminiscent of those Bulls-Pistons battles. In fact, the Knicks and wily coach Pat Riley devised some anti-Jordan defensive schemes that rekindled memories of Chuck Daly and his Jordan Rules. The Knicks held service, winning the first two games at home with Jordan experiencing shooting problems and John Starks coming right at his face. For all practical purposes, the Bulls faced a do-or-die situation coming home to the Stadium for game three. Jordan had an off-night and still the Bulls salvaged this critical game. In game four, everyone sensed that Michael would rise to the occasion. Jordan whipped up on the New Yorkers for 54 points in a resounding 105-95 victory. He dropped in six three-pointers while converting 18-of-30 shots from the floor and 12-of-14 free throws.

"When he gets like that, it doesn't really matter what else happens," said Bulls coach Phil Jackson. "He puts on a show of his own, and he's in a different space than everyone else."

"He was passing the ball today—passing it right to the basket," Riley said. "Michael was in a zone and had everything going for him. John Starks had a hand in his face, but it didn't matter."

Properly inspired, the Bulls won the next two, in effect sweeping four in a row from the trash-talking, physical Knicks. In the clincher, Jordan was the ultimate team player with a final line of 29 points, 10 rebounds, and 14 assists.

Chicago entered the Finals against Phoenix, which featured a mega-star of its own in Charles Barkley. The Bulls began their three-peat quest as if they were going to blow the Suns out, capturing the first two games on Phoenix's homecourt. Jordan's 31 points and

Scottie Pippen's 27 led to a 100-92 victory. This win was followed by a 111-108 decision two days later, with Jordan garnering 42 points, 12 rebounds, and nine assists. Despite Michael's 44 points back in Chicago, the Suns stunned the Bulls 129-121 in game three—a nail-biting affair that went into triple overtime. Just to be sure that didn't happen again, Michael went off for 55 points in leading the Bulls to a 111-105 triumph in game four and a seemingly insurmountable 3-1 series lead.

Demonstrating the heart of a championship-caliber team for the first time in the Finals, the Suns bounced back with a 108-98 victo-ry in game five. The city of Chicago had put extra police on alert and stores had boarded up windows in anticipation of a Bulls victory and citywide revelry. "We did the city a favor," Barkley said. "You can take all those boards down now. We're going back to Phoenix."

It was at the America West Arena where the Bulls became three-time champions. Down by two in the waning moments, John Paxson hit a dramatic three-pointer with three seconds left. Horace Grant then blocked Kevin Johnson's drive, and the final horn sounded. Jordan's 33 points gave him a Finals average of 41.0, a new record. He raced into the crowd for the game ball after

Opposite: Jordan drives with determination around New York's John Starks. *This page, left:* The Suns' Danny Ainge knows you just can't defend when Michael is hot. *Above:* Solo flight. MJ was on fire against Phoenix in the '93 Finals.

Grant's block and then collected his third Finals MVP trophy, becoming the first player to accomplish that feat. No other player has ever won even two in a row.

"When my kids grow older and other people's kids grow older, I'll look back on winning three championships and be most proud of it," Jordan said. "You look at the Celtics

who won 16 championships, and they certainly must be considered a great team. But with so much talent and parity in the league right now, we certainly feel we must be considered one of the greatest teams."

If we had listened more carefully, been more sensitive to Michael Jordan the person rather than selfishly demanding more and expecting to be thrilled and entertained by Michael the entertainer—we would have seen the telltale signs. They were there all along throughout the season. Had we been more aware of Michael's own feelings and needs, the announcement of his retirement would not have been such a shock. There were a select few in the media who wrote columns during the playoffs speculating that MJ could call it quits after a three-peat title.

Had we paid attention, here's what we would have seen: Michael had always said that the moment he detected a waning of his skills, when lesser lights in the NBA began staying with him and occasionally surpassing him, it would be time to bid a hasty farewell. Jordan was a spectacular rookie late in Julius Erving's career, and he watched intently as players with half the Doctor's skills in his prime would almost embarrass him on the court. Jordan vowed to himself, and confided to those close to him, that he would never let that happen to him.

The first sign of a slight erosion was Jordan's shooting percentage, which had taken a dip to 49.6 percent in 1992-93 after remaining above 50 percent for the five previous seasons. The thinking was that Jordan was attempting more difficult shots in trying to carry the team during various points in the season, and that may be true. Yet, and only Michael knows for certain, some of those degree-of-difficulty attempts that were missing now used to drop for him with unreal regularity.

The physical beating was finally beginning to take its cumulative toll—the ankle injury against Atlanta in the first round of the playoffs; the wrist injury against the Knicks in the Eastern Conference finals; the sprained left foot in the regular season. Jordan has always been a unique physical marvel, an anomaly in that despite the terrific stress and strain he continually put on his body, he only suffered one serious injury in nine years, and that was purely by accident. Had he landed normally on his left foot in 1985 at Golden State, he would

Opposite, left: Younger players like John Starks tried to defend against Jordan by egging him into verbal and physical scuffles. **Right:** Proving you're the fastest gun in the West takes its toll.

have had near-perfect attendance in his career. With only 3.8 percent body fat and the addition of a solid weightlifting program to his regimen, Jordan should have been stronger than ever. But maybe something happens to the body, even one as magnificent as Michael's, when you turn 30. The smaller injuries don't heal as quickly; the body doesn't recuperate as fast for back-to-back games.

There was also the case of John Starks. Certainly a talented, if inconsistent, player in his own right, Starks bullied and scraped and fought with Jordan during a hellacious playoff series, conning the league's ultimate con man into one-on-one skirmishes that aided the Knicks and hurt the Bulls. This had to play on Jordan's mind. There would only be more like John Starks coming into the NBA each season, looking to make a name for themselves by staying with the top gun. They would have youth and a fresh supply of talent on their side with nothing to lose. Jordan would be expected to put the young bucks in their place, and if he slipped, the media would make it a big deal. It would be like the days in the Wild West. The fastest gun had to continually prove he was quicker and more accurate, lest he get shown up at sundown.

These had to be some of the thoughts going through Michael's mind as he took up a seemingly personal crusade to bring a third-straight title to Chicago. Put in this light, the accomplishment seems all the more significant. Winning the third title made the Bulls arguably the second-greatest NBA team of

October 5, 1993, started out as a glorious night for Chicago sports. The White Sox were playing their first playoff game in 10 years, and Michael Jordan threw out the first pitch. Throughout the game, though, rumors started to fly that Jordan had decided to retire from basketball. Later that evening, media broadcast the news to a shocked and disbelieving audience.

all-time, trailing only the eight-time champion Boston Celtics of the 1960s. Having assured the Bulls' place in history and having carved his niche one rung higher than repeat NBA champs Magic Johnson and Isiah Thomas and surpassing Larry Bird—who never won two consecutive—Jordan could finally rest.

Something Michael cherished but had never wanted to reveal was his special friendship with four young kids in a tough area of Chicago's West Side. Jordan regularly visited the kids after home games, and he eventually demanded to see their report cards to check on their progress in school. It might have remained Michael's secret except

that a couple of Bulls fans had their car break down one night across the street from where Jordan held his get-togethers. They noticed Jordan's car and then saw him talking with the youths.

"It was really a thing with Michael," said his wife Juanita. "I think Michael became concerned that his visits were beginning to take over their lives. So, he asked to see their grades to check and see if they were paying attention to their schoolwork."

Early in the season, *Forbes* magazine released its third-annual ranking of the world's highest-paid athletes, and Michael topped the list with an estimated income of $35.9 million. That broke down to $32

million in endorsements and the $3.9 million paid to him by the Bulls. His biggest endorsement contract was for $20 million with Nike, the most lucrative in the sport world.

Jordan's immense fame continued to force an almost Elvis-like lifestyle upon him, a prisoner to hotel rooms and charter jets. "People are lined up in every hotel lobby to see him," said the Bulls' director of media Tim Hallam. "We got to a Washington hotel one night at 3 a.m. and 75 people were there. Parents and their kids—at three in the morning!"

Hallam said that the morning after Jordan sprained his wrist in game two of the Bulls-Knicks playoff series, he received 20 phone calls before 7 A.M. The Bulls-Cavaliers series produced 278 phone messages on Hallam's answering machine. "I counted them," he said. "Do you know how long a tape that is?"

Hallam said that Jordan had considered wearing a disguise so he could get out, which is difficult when you're 6'6". Michael gave it a shot once in St. Louis and was uncovered within five minutes.

Michael Jordan's restaurant officially opened in May 1993. Early patrons included NBC-TV's Ahmad Rashad, Magic Johnson, Chicago Bears' star Richard Dent, and Charles Barkley. Three-hour waits weren't uncommon, and the telephone company reported 5,800 busy signals in one day. Jordan has a private section off the main dining room where he entertains guests.

"The food's pretty good," Barkley said, "but not as good as Majerle's." Suns teammate Dan Majerle owns a sports bar in Phoenix. "Next time he comes in, it won't be for free," Jordan shot back.

Michael and Barkley have forged a strong bond in their personal lives

that could be witnessed even on the field of competition. Although they are two very different people, their high visibility in the public eye—garnered in part from their skills on the court—gives them a common ground.

"He [Jordan] has said some things that inspired me, private things not in the media, just whispering," Sir Charles once said. "A lot of the media are on my bandwagon now, but a couple of times when we played in the playoffs and lost, he

Opposite: **We are amused! Sirs Michael and Charles prove you can be friends on and off the court.** *Above:* **Media and fans are always anxious to hear anything Michael has to say. There seems to be no end to the constant clamoring for "just one more question."**

told me to hang in there, that I'd one day be on a team good enough to win. I appreciated that. He was there for me when things were not going good. That's the sign of a friend."

OFF THE COURT

Above: **Three of the most familiar faces in the world—Michael, Charles Barkley, and Mickey Mouse.** *Opposite:* **Looking dapper in his tux, MJ strikes a pose for the camera while attending a benefit dinner for the Michael Jordan Foundation.**

Michael Jordan himself could have never imagined the fame and fortune that would come his way for being the greatest basketball player ever. In the beginning, he thoroughly enjoyed all the trappings and luxuries that his stardom and new-found wealth could deliver. To help break up the monotony of preseason bus rides to games, for example, Jordan bought a huge portable stereo with speakers big and loud enough for a mansion.

It was like that with the cars he bought, the furs and jewelry he wore that he would later put away. In his early NBA years, he didn't mind calling attention to himself. Later, he preferred to remain out of the public's eye.

There is something unique about Jordan, a presence that goes beyond the Baryshnikov-like hang time and the aerial ballet that have made him the best-known basketball player in the world. It starts with his personality—warm, outgoing, genuine.

Joking with him at his locker room stall, sitting with him in a restaurant, watching him shoot some pool in his basement, these are the times you come to know the real man. There doesn't seem to be anything artificial about the guy. He can afford to be anybody he wants, of course, with the millions of dollars fattening his bank account each year. With all that temptation to "become" something else, we appreciate all the more how he managed to stay true to himself.

Michael's Midas touch—or maybe that should be amended to the Michael Touch—begins with the Bulls' contract that pays him close to $4 million a year. Add to that the estimated $30 million he nets in endorsements each year. Gatorade signed an $18 million, 10-year deal with him after Coca-Cola decided not to renew its endorsement agreement. Arnold Palmer had been the kingpin of the endorsement buck among sports figures, but Jordan surpassed him after the Bulls won their first NBA title. Michael's clients have included McDonald's, Wheaties, Nike, Chevrolet, Wilson Sporting Goods, Johnson Products, and the Illinois State Lottery. He also has had limited real estate partnerships in Miami; Kansas City; San Clemente, California; and Washington, D.C. He has owned land in Hilton Head, South Carolina. Most recently, he opened a restaurant in Chicago that bears a monster-size portrait of the King of the Court preparing to slam-jam one in the basket. His appeal is so strong that his mother, Deloris, did TV commercials for Empire Carpeting in Chicago.

Michael is represented by ProServ, a Washington-based sports management group. Senior vice-president David Falk has been overseeing Jordan's financial empire from day one. Rather than the shotgun approach taken by other sports celebrities such as former Chicago Bears coach Mike Ditka, Falk advocated carefully selecting only those corporations and products that best reflected the image Jordan portrays. In the case of McDonald's, Jordan does swear by the fast-food conglomerate. He's been consuming Big Macs since he was old enough to walk up to the counter.

In 1984, Jordan had just finished a workout with the Olympic team when coach Bobby Knight came in and told several of the players they'd been drafted by NBA teams. He asked how they would commemorate such an occasion, and most of the players said they'd be dining at expensive restaurants, running up exorbitant tabs, and toasting with Dom Perignon. "Well Jordan, you were the third player picked. What are you going to do to celebrate?" Knight asked. "I'm going down to McDonald's and ordering three Big Macs, with fries and a large Coke," Michael said with a grin. According to Knight, that's exactly what the North Carolina star did. It's little wonder McDonald's came out with a limited edition of the McJordan burger.

"Michael Jordan continues to exceed everyone's expectations of him, whether it's on the basketball court or in the marketing arena," Falk said. "By matching him with some of the cornerstones of American marketing—Nike, McDonald's, Coca-Cola, Wheaties—we've created a real synergy which ties each of the companies together and further enhances his name recognition."

ProServ's deal with Nike actually saved that shoe company from a possible bankruptcy, as more than 60,000 pairs of Air Jordan gym shoes were purchased in the first three months of their introduction. Sales have long since gone into the millions with Michael reaping a generous percentage. Those shoes today are sold for more than $100 a pair, and kids can't buy them fast enough. At its peak, wearing Air Jordans became a fashion statement, the ultimate in cool footwear.

Jordan would be given an endless supply of complimentary shoes along with sweats, shorts, T-shirts, socks, warmups, and other Nike sports apparel. He would wear a brand-new pair of shoes for each game, initially breaking them in during shoot-around practices eight hours prior to tipoff. After the games, he would give away his shoes to various charities, the ball-boys, or friends.

Opposite: Kids love Michael—and he loves them. Here, a pair of his famous footwear gets passed along to some very lucky fans. *This page, above:* Th-th-that's all, folks! Michael mugged with Bugs and Porky during a commercial spot for Nike. *Right:* Multi-talented Michael spies an opportunity to toss one into the end zone.

Jordan is extremely loyal to the products he endorses, realizing that the better they sell, the more money he eventually makes—as if he needs any more! He'll walk up to a pop machine and if there isn't any Coke, he'll scan the choices to see if there are any Coca-Cola products. He refuses to drink Pepsi. It's the same with shoes. He constantly chides anyone wearing a competitive brand, and is especially rough with Reebok wearers, which is Nike's primary competition.

Michael's popularity was at an all-time high even as he announced his retirement the first week of October 1993. He continued to endorse major products during his minor-league baseball days in 1994.

What he represents is a slice of life in the best of America's tradition, the small-town boy who made it big. Michael has gone from his self-described "goony-looking" high school portrait to the covers of *GQ, Esquire, Newsweek, Sports Illustrated,* and numerous other publications. He has made guest appearances on the *Tonight Show, Arsenio Hall Show, David Letterman,* and *Good Morning America.* He was even featured on *60 Minutes* and was once the guest host for *Saturday Night Live.* Originally it was hoped he'd accept a part in the movie *Heaven Is a Playground,* but he had to back out when actual filming took more than a year to get arranged.

Michael's summer of 1988 was filled with a dozen appearances to participate in various pro-am golf tournaments around the country. Barbara Allen was Michael's appointments manager, and it was a full-time job just trying to keep pace with one of the world's busiest celebrities. He was a guest on *The Today Show* in New York and later that day accepted the Seagram's Award as the league's top player. He spent time working at his basketball camp in North Carolina and also the one at Illinois Benedictine College in Lisle, a suburb west of Chicago. His Chicago-area camp has since been relocated.

Other activities that summer included leading the annual Bud

Opposite: How 'bout a game of one-on-one with The Man? **This page, top:** Michael and two big Macs. At the Ronald McDonald Golf Outing, Mike pairs up with Jim McMahon and Ronald McDonald to raise funds. **Below:** Fore! An avid golfer, MJ loves the challenge of the links.

Billiken Day Parade in Chicago; taking part in the Special Olympics Summer Games at Notre Dame; and coaching Patrick Ewing, James Worthy, and Dominique Wilkins in a three-on-three exhibition game against three winners of a national drawing. Michael finally took time off for a European vacation that included stops in Italy and Monte Carlo.

Later that year he headed up the first annual McDonald's Golf Invitational in west suburban Lemont, Illinois, to raise money for the Ronald McDonald House charity. There were 117 celebrities of various kinds who participated in the event along with many top executives from major corporations in Chicago. The outing raised more than $50,000 and included Jordan, sports announcer Brent Musburger, and former Chicago Bears superstar running backs Walter Payton and Gale Sayers. The tournament received front-page coverage and was the highlight of the television news that night.

You may have noticed his affinity for the game of golf. The sport that cannot be completely mastered provides the ultimate challenge for a multitalented athlete with an endless burning desire to compete. What both frustrates and fascinates Jordan is golf's unpredictability and how he can never control the game. He is fond of saying he can make free throws practically anytime he wants. Even those triple-pump,

over-the-shoulder, double-reverse, topspin-off-the-glass layups would fall in more often than some of Jordan's putts, even though he is a six-handicap golfer. He once said that after he retires from the NBA, he would like to join the Senior PGA Tour.

It appears that Jordan first got interested in golf while in college, learning the game from a fellow Tar Heel, Davis Love III, now a PGA Tour golfer. Michael can drive the ball long distances with accuracy. The part of his game that is his weakest is probably his irons.

He did have fun with his public. During the league's All-Star Weekend in Miami in 1989, he went golfing with PGA Tour star Raymond Floyd and close friend Scott Gitlitz, whose family owns the Deerfield Multiplex Fitness Club in Illinois where the Bulls practiced until 1992. They drove to a somewhat remote, private course where Jordan figured he could shoot a peaceful game, relax, and enjoy himself. Of course, as usual, somebody discovered his presence. Two young boys, their mouths wide open, crept up slowly on Jordan & Co., perhaps not quite sure how to react. Working up the nerve, they started to approach Jordan to ask for an autograph. Sensing an opportunity for a little playful fun, Jordan hopped in his golf cart and sped away, the boys giving chase. This went on for a while with Jordan making like Mario Andretti, laughing up a storm as the kids gave futile chase.

Jordan's tremendous popularity is not limited to the boundaries of the United States. He has become an equally huge phenomenon overseas, particularly in Europe, where basketball is a fast-growing sport. After a recent visit to Holland, American tourists came home wide-eyed with tales of Dutch teenagers

wearing all manner of Jordan paraphernalia, imitating his basketball moves right down to hanging their tongues out. A Bulls playoff game on television in the town of Huizen was treated like a national holiday. Maarten Hendriks, 17, telephoned all the way to Chicago in June 1993 to inquire when the Bulls-Phoenix game was scheduled. Since Holland is seven hours ahead of Chicago time, Hendriks calculated that the NBA Finals showdown game would be televised in Holland at 1 a.m. since it was being shown at 6 p.m. on a Sunday at Chicago Stadium. With that, Hendriks took a nap from 8 p.m. until tipoff, woke up when his alarm went off, and sat down to

watch his main man light up the Suns.

In Germany, an American girl stared in disbelief when a young German teenage boy walked past her with his head shaved and only the initials "MJ" standing out. The American girl lived in Germany for three years and experienced the

Above: **Michael mania knows no bounds. Fans of all ages and from all over the world want to be like Mike. A very accommodating MJ tries to sign as many autographs as possible, even while in transit.** *Opposite:* **Shadow dancing. Flight 23, now departing for takeoff.**

Deutsche version of Jordanmania first hand. "The kids at Vogelweh Air Force Base dressed like him, acted like him, wore his wristbands, kneepads, shoes, and Air Jordan T-shirts," said Joyce Okamoto. "The basketball players on our school team tried to do his dunks. Kids would come to class all red-eyed in the morning after staying up until 4 a.m. to watch a Bulls game. They'd look up his past, where he went to school. They'd cut out all the pictures and articles of him in newspapers and magazines and put them all over their lockers. Kids would beg and plead for a Michael Jordan poster."

The love kids have for Michael is returned liberally from MJ. No. 23 is crazy about kids, now the father to three of his own. There are times when he'll simply cancel all appointments and scheduled outings, retreat to his home, and play with the kids. After one such fun-filled afternoon, wife Juanita confessed she wasn't sure who were the kids and who was the father. Michael and Juanita were married in 1989 in what was to be a secret ceremony in Las Vegas. As it usually does, word leaked out and the groom was blitzed with autograph requests instead of being bombarded with rice on his way to the bridal limousine.

The couple first met at a postgame gathering in Bennigan's on Michigan Avenue in Chicago one night after a game in Michael's rookie year. Juanita was a secretary for a downtown firm and wasn't a big pro basketball fan. She had little idea the man she was talking to was the Bulls' franchise. "That's what I liked about her, that she cared about me as a person and not because I played for the Bulls," Jordan said. "People may think this sounds crazy, but it was sometimes hard for me to meet the right girls.

Opposite, top and bottom: **Michael and Juanita Jordan enjoy themselves at events where they can share a laugh with pals like Magic Johnson and raise money for a good cause.** *This page, above:* **Some of MJ's V.I.P.'s—Juanita and Jeffery Jordan.** *Top, right:* **Mike throws out the first pitch at the Chicago White Sox postseason game in '93.** *Bottom:* **Mr. Jordan makes a fashion statement.**

You're always wondering if they just want to be with you because you're a pro player and make a lot of money. How can you really be sure they like you for who you are? I tried to be very careful about who I went out with."

Being a world-famous celebrity isn't always fun and games. It eventually wore Jordan down and frustrated him because he is normally a person who loves to mingle with people. An ordinary errand, such as shopping for furniture, becomes a big deal if you're in his shoes. What Michael used to do is call up an exclusive Scandinavian furniture store and make arrangements to visit after hours. That way, he could browse and make his selections without having to sign a hundred or so autographs along the way.

He's been known to do his formal shopping in Paris, where he once purchased 18 business suits. When it comes to meetings with corporate heads and CEOs, Jordan has just the right look. At one time, he would wear nonprescription business glasses to lend a more seri-

ous, businesslike look to his financial meetings. Jordan's appearance fee for one hour has exceeded $15,000, and yet sometimes he is still forced to turn down requests for lack of time.

In between promotional appearances, filming commercials, and charity appearances for the children at the St. Jude's Research Hospital in Memphis, a typical Jordan off-season would be filled to the brim with golf events. During the Federal Express-St. Jude Classic Pro-Am in Memphis, he took time off to visit with the kids at St. Jude's. "Michael reaches out with his heart to children with special needs," mom Deloris Jordan said. "You know, it really does make him feel good that he can have that effect on kids, and the kids just love him. Those sick children look up to Michael, and

I think it gives them some hope to make their wishes come true."

Before he started the Michael Jordan Foundation, he worked with the Starlight Foundation, a group that arranges last wishes for terminally ill children. Jordan will never forget the young boy who came to visit him before a game and then sat on the Bulls' bench during the game. Jordan spent quite a bit of time with him and did his best to encourage him in his fight against leukemia. Some months later, Jordan asked the Starlight woman how the youngster was doing. She didn't know how to respond at first. Eventually, she told Michael that the boy had died earlier that week. The look on Jordan's face was one of shock, followed by sadness. He has since backed away from doing such requests because of the emo-

Above: **The Michael Jordan Foundation is one of Mike's pet projects. Whenever possible, he makes time to spend with the kids.** *Opposite:* **Adding a pair of glasses enhances Michael's business image.**

tional connection he makes with kids and realizing what the end holds in store. Jordan has helped so many people in his lifetime, and that feeling of helplessness when a child is dying was more than he could bear.

Perhaps the most tragic event ever to happen in Michael's life was the death of his beloved 56-year-old father James in North Carolina last summer. Michael inherited his sense of responsibility and intelligence from his mother. From his father came the mischievous, fun-loving personality and the smile that could light up Wilmington,

North Carolina. James Jordan was not only his dad, but also his best friend. James Jordan knew how to make others laugh, a gift he had passed onto his son. In a low voice, Michael spoke of how special James was to the five Jordan kids, and how they now appreciated Mom and Dad setting goals for their children. A college education was always stressed. "Don't dwell on his death, but celebrate the life he lived," Michael said, struggling at times to hold back the emotion bottled up inside.

Michael initially developed his ultra-competitive nature—one of the characteristics that has driven him to such heights—when he was growing up. Like all superstars, he hates to lose. At anything. He will persevere against superior Ping-Pong players, refusing to stop until he wins a game or two.

During the Bulls' 1985 training camp at Beloit College in Wisconsin, the team took a day off for a golf outing with corporate sponsors and the media. After a steak dinner, Jordan began hustling on the pool table, taking on all comers at $5 a game. One by one, his opponents succumbed as Michael was laughing, talking, and sinking shots, psyching out opponents with his chatter.

A 10-year-old boy who was very good took Jordan on, and the kid had one run of four balls. Jordan smiled, but then turned a little more serious. It came down to the final ball, which Michael sunk. The little boy put his head down when Jordan asked him for the $5. He dug deep in his pocket, pulled it out, and handed it over. Jordan gave him a serious look and reminded him that gambling in life

meant he'd better be ready to pay the price if he lost.

Finally came the biggest challenge of the night. The local pool shark stepped forward and began connecting his professional-looking, personalized cue stick. By the ease and dexterity the player demonstrated as he warmed up, Jordan knew he was in for a battle. The audience of 75 or 80 people began buzzing that the cocky Chicagoan would

finally meet his match. Jordan and the man went at one another like Paul Newman and Jackie Gleason in the movie *The Hustler*. This was crunch time, North Carolina vs. Georgetown, Magic vs. Michael. It came down to a difficult shot that if Michael missed, the game was over.

There was a look of total concentration on Jordan's face as he lined up the shot. It was the same kind of intensity he would display six months later in hitting two free throws with time expired to force a second overtime in a playoff to Boston. Jordan took a deep breath and let the cue stick glide smoothly through his long fingers. Stick met cue ball just right, sending the winning shot on its way to the corner pocket.

Jordan pumped his right fist three times, the same gesture that would haunt Cleveland Cavalier fans in 1989 when his last-second shot would eliminate the favored Cavs from the playoffs. The locals marveled at how this basketball player had beaten their best. Jordan was a gracious winner, complimenting his opponent and saying how fortunate he had been. When the subject of a rematch was broached, Jordan begged off, realizing he had beaten a superior opponent and there was no sense pressing his luck.

As for the 10-year-old boy? Jordan had him rack the balls for that final match and gave him $5 for the chore. The kid walked away with an ear-to-ear smile. His faith in his hero had been restored.

Opposite: **A guiding force in Michael's life, he gives his family credit for shaping him into the person he is today. Michael cited his father as responsible for giving him his sense of humor. Here the two enjoy a laugh on the golf course in '91.** *This page:* **The familiar clenched-fist triple-pump carries into Mike's golf game, too.**

A WHOLE NEW ERA

Opposite: **Mike strikes back! Michael Jordan shoots past rival Reggie Miller during the celebrated Jordan comeback game, March 19, 1995.** *Above:* **MJ shakes Antonio Davis and deals.**

I'm back."

With these two words, Michael Jordan ended his almost 18-month hiatus from professional basketball and started a new era for the Chicago Bulls. It was an interlude that saw Michael tackle the challenge of fulfilling his lifelong dream of playing professional baseball and saw his own popularity reach dizzying new heights.

On October 6, 1993, Michael announced that he was retiring from professional basketball. One sensed that the media pressure had gotten to Jordan following the death of his father, James. As Michael said on the day he retired, "I've always stressed to people that have known me and the media that has followed me that when I lose the sense of motivation and the sense to prove something as a basketball player, it's time for me to move away from the game of basketball."

As the shock of that fateful day was sinking in to the millions of Jordan fans worldwide, reports that at the time seemed odd started circulating: Jordan was daily, for hours on end, taking batting practice and fielding practice in the basement of Comiskey Park or at Illinois Institute of Technology. There were times that his batting practice was supervised by the White Sox' guru of hitting, batting coach Walt Hriniak. And it wasn't just that Michael was trying his luck

toward eventually playing the senior golf circuit, since he had become so fanatical about golf. But baseball had been his first love growing up, and it was the sport that he and his father had shared.

"The way he played baseball in Little League, he made me become a fan," James had said. "If I wouldn't take him to play ball, he'd look so pitiful, like he'd lost every friend in the world and was all by himself. You'd take one look at him and say, 'OK, let's go.' He would do things in baseball and excel beyond kids his age that you would just get caught up in it."

Edward Lewis, the varsity baseball coach at E.A. Laney High School, told *USA Today Baseball Weekly* that he didn't even know that Jordan was going to go out for basketball until Michael was a sophomore. Until that point, Lewis said, Jordan was known only as a baseball player. As a junior in high school, Jordan pitched more than 40 scoreless innings while batting in the No. 5 or No. 6 hole in the lineup. Two games into his senior year in baseball, Michael was invited to play basketball in the McDonald's high school all-star game. To do so would mean that he would have to forfeit his remaining eligibility as a baseball player. Michael decided to play in the all-star game.

It would be more than a dozen years before Michael would play in another competitive baseball game. Jordan had developed a fine relationship with Chicago Bulls owner Jerry Reinsdorf, who is also owner of the Chicago White Sox. Reinsdorf's dealings with Jordan had been—almost without exception—amicable (especially when compared to some of Reinsdorf's dealings with other Bulls players). Michael announced his retirement from the Bulls but did not sever his relationship with

Above: **Michael Jordan's fierce determination was evident every day during 1994 spring training with the White Sox.** *Opposite:* **Nowhere did that persistence pay off more than at the plate. He took extra batting practice (as well as extra fielding practice), and by the time he was finished in the Arizona Fall League, he batted .252.**

in some batting cages. He was hitting 600 to 1,000 balls a day and studying tapes of hitters such as Frank Thomas. It seemed impossible, but rumors agreed that Michael was going to play professional baseball.

Many of Michael's friends and fans thought that he might work

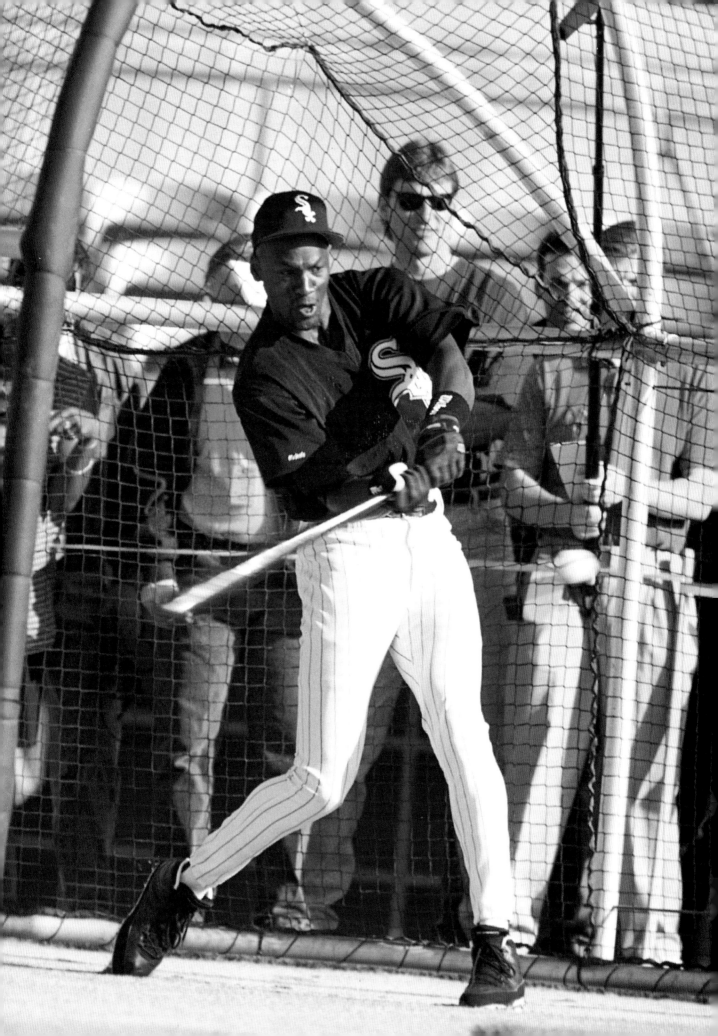

Reinsdorf. Thus, on February 7, 1994, the White Sox signed Michael to a minor-league contract.

The skeptics immediately raised the roof. "A million-to-one shot," was the consensus among the commentators. Of course, those were odds that Jordan was willing to take. "He won't be able to take the 12-hour bus rides," the fans on call-in shows intoned. Michael is 6'6", and he was used to flying to games as the best basketball player in history, so he went out and bought his team a more roomy bus. He is, after all, Michael Jordan.

There are no shortcuts to becoming a good hitter, Jordan told everyone as he donned his baseball gear early in the season. And as Mike Lum, the roving hitting instructor for the White Sox minor-league system, told *USA Today Baseball Weekly*, "I know a lot of people aren't taking [Michael]

seriously, but if they could be around him and see his work ethic, they would change their minds. He is always out early for extra batting practice. He was on the field at 7:30 every morning during spring training. He wants to learn."

Jordan's fans, however, wanted only to see their hero up-close. From spring training in Florida to games with the Double-A Birmingham Bulls during the season to the Arizona Fall League for top prospects, enthusiastic fans filled stands and cheered Jordan's every move. The Birmingham franchise and other teams in the Southern League broke several attendance records, and some say that Jordan's presence might have preserved the Arizona Fall League's existence.

Michael was present, however, only to become a professional baseball player. His raw numbers for his lone season at Double-A

don't jump out at you. He batted .202 with three homers and 51 runs batted in in 436 at bats. But a closer look reveals that he was becoming a real prospect. He batted .260 in the last four weeks of the season, and he totaled 30 stolen bases, good for fifth in the Southern League. While playing with baseball's top prospects in the fall, Michael made another stride, batting .252. All agreed that it was amazing for anyone who hadn't played baseball in a dozen years to come into pro ball and compete right away at such a high level. It wasn't just anyone who did it, however. It was Michael Jordan.

As did other minor leaguers in 1995, Jordan reported to spring training, anxious to renew his bid to become a major-league player. Michael had been working very hard in the off-season to prepare for the 1995 campaign. He thought that this was to be his breakthrough season. Michael was in all likelihood going to report to Triple-A Nashville after spring training. Many experts thought that if he continued to make the same kind of progress that he did while he was a Double-A player, he would get a call-up in September, if not sooner. There was a new obstacle in Michael's way, however: the strike.

Major-league players went on strike in August 1994, and there was no break in the negotiations. Jordan refused to comment on the overall labor situation, preferring to concentrate on the aspects of his game that needed improvement. He also knew that anything he said might come back to haunt him.

Ron Schueler, the White Sox general manager, wasn't so reticent,

"I know a lot of people aren't taking [Michael] seriously, but if they could be around him and see his work ethic, they would change their minds."
—Mike Lum, White Sox hitting instructor

however. Baseball management decided to play spring training games with both minor leaguers and replacement players, while the Players Association maintained that any player participating in a "big-league" spring training game was breaking the strike. Jordan has strong union leanings, and along with other top baseball prospects he decided that it would be in his best long-term interests not to cross the

picket line to play in a spring training game with replacement players. In early March of 1995, Schueler told White Sox minor leaguers who refused to play in spring training games to pack their gear and move it from the major-league clubhouse to the minor-league facility. Michael packed his gear and moved it to his car.

A week later, Jordan issued a statement announcing that he was retiring from baseball. He knew that his progress on the diamond had to

Opposite: **The trademark quick first step that he utilized to blow past the best defensive basketball players in the world—such as Joe Dumars and Michael Cooper—also helped MJ become quite a base thief. He swiped 30 bags for Birmingham.** *Above:* **Down on the farm: Jordan** *(right)* **and a fan take time out for our National Anthem.**

be made at a fairly rapid rate. He also knew that any opportunity the strike cost him seriously hampered his chances to move to the major-league level.

Jordan had an opportunity in basketball, though, with a standing offer to show up at Bulls' practices and work out with the team. After he had hung up his spikes and returned from Florida in mid-March, Michael appeared at the Bulls' training facility several times. The media swarm—which had seemed to be dissipating after he had played a full year of minor-league ball—returned and jammed the Berto Center day after day until March 18, 1995. That was the day that Michael said those two little words that Bulls fans and basketball lovers all over the world wanted to hear.

"I'm back."

His first game back on the hard courts was on March 19 in Indianapolis against the Pacers. One of the premier teams in the Eastern Conference, Indiana boasted one of the best shooting guards in basketball and a long-time rival of Jordan's, Reggie Miller. When Michael first walked out onto

the court at Market Square Arena, he was wearing No. 45—the number he wore as a baseball player. His old No. 23 hung in the rafters of Chicago's United Center, having been retired at the beginning of the season. "I really didn't want to bring that number down," Michael said, "because that's the last thing that my father saw me in.

"It's a whole new era right now," he continued. "Forty-five kind of gives me a fresh start."

Michael's return to basketball ended with him garnering 19 points, six assists, and six rebounds in 43 minutes. His conditioning wasn't up to par—which could be expected, considering that the March 19 game was in effect his first preseason game.

Why did Michael come back? "I love the game," he said after his historic return. "I had a good opportunity to come back. . . . I think at the time I walked away from it, I probably needed [the break], mentally more so than anything. But I really, truly missed the game. I missed my friends. I certainly missed my teammates."

And everybody knows that Sir

Michael, the Air to the Throne, is good for basketball, just as he was for baseball. It was estimated that his return to the court would generate hundreds of millions of dollars for all the companies affiliated with Jordan and the NBA. Moreover, Michael's return would likely improve the image of the NBA, which had become tarnished by the antics of a few of its spoiled young stars.

"Quite frankly, I really felt I wanted to instill some positive things back in the game," Jordan said. "There's a lot of negative things that have been happening. . . . The Larry Birds and the Magic Johnsons and the Doctor Js, all those players . . . paved the road for a lot of young guys. And the young guys are not taking care of their responsibility for maintaining that love for the game. I just think you should respect the game."

Top: **Three legends: Bobby Knight** *(from right),* **Dean Smith, and MJ at Michael's number-retiring ceremony.** *Above:* **Scottie Pippen and Michael face off during Pippen's charity game in September 1994.** *Opposite:* **He's baaack!**

JORDAN BY THE NUMBERS

NBA REGULAR-SEASON STATISTICS

		G	MIN	FG	PCT	FG	PCT	FT	PCT	OFF	TOT	AST	STL	BLK	PTS	PPG
				—FGs—		3-PT FGs		—FTs—		Rebounds						
84-85	CHI	82	3144	837	.515	9	.173	630	.845	167	534	481	196	69	*2313	28.2
85-86	CHI	18	451	150	.457	3	.167	105	.840	23	64	53	37	21	408	22.7
86-87	CHI	82	*3281	*1098	.482	12	.182	*833	.857	166	430	377	236	125	*3041	*37.1
87-88	CHI	82	*3311	*1069	.535	7	.132	*723	.841	139	449	485	*259	131	*2868	*35.0
88-89	CHI	81	*3255	*966	.538	27	.276	674	.850	149	652	650	234	65	*2633	*32.5
89-90	CHI	82	*3197	*1034	.526	92	.376	593	.848	143	565	519	*227	54	*2753	*33.6
90-91	CHI	82	3034	*990	.539	29	.312	571	.851	118	492	453	223	83	*2580	*31.5
91-92	CHI	80	3102	*943	.519	27	.270	491	.832	91	511	489	182	75	*2404	*30.0
92-93	CHI	78	3067	*992	.495	81	.352	476	.837	135	522	428	*221	61	*2541	*32.6
Totals		667	25842	8079	.516	287	.301	5096	.846	1131	4219	3935	1815	684	21541	32.3

* Led league.

NBA REGULAR-SEASON ACHIEVEMENTS

- Holds career NBA record for scoring average, 32.3.
- Ranks 6th in career steals, 1,815.
- Ranks 15th in career points, 21,541.
- Scored the 3rd most points in a season, 3,041 in 1986-87.
- Recorded the 5th highest scoring average in a season, 37.1 in 1986-87.
- Tallied the 9th most points in a game, 69 on March 28, 1990.
- Recorded the 2nd most steals in a game, 10 on January 29, 1988.
- Tied with Wilt Chamberlain for the most consecutive scoring titles, seven.
- Scored the most consecutive points in a game, 23 on April 16, 1987.
- Won gold medal as a member of the 1992 U.S. Olympic team.

WORLD CHAMPIONSHIPS
1991	1992	1993

NBA FINALS MVP
1991	1992	1993

NBA MOST VALUABLE PLAYER
1987-88	1990-91	1991-92

NBA ROOKIE OF THE YEAR
1984-85

NBA DEFENSIVE PLAYER OF THE YEAR
1987-88

ALL-NBA FIRST TEAM
1986-87	1990-91
1987-88	1991-92
1988-89	1992-93
1989-90	

NBA ALL-DEFENSIVE FIRST TEAM
1987-88	1990-91
1988-89	1991-92
1989-90	1992-93

NBA PLAYOFF STATISTICS

		G	MIN	—FGs— FG	PCT	3-PT FGs FG	PCT	—FTs— FT	PCT	Rebounds OFF	TOT	AST	STL	BLK	PTS	PPG
84-85	CHI	4	171	34	.436	1	.125	48	.828	7	23	34	11	4	117	29.3
85-86	CHI	3	135	48	.505	1	1.00	34	.872	5	19	17	7	4	131	43.7
86-87	CHI	3	128	35	.417	2	.400	35	.897	7	21	18	6	7	107	35.7
87-88	CHI	10	427	138	.531	1	.333	86	.869	23	71	47	24	11	363	36.3
88-89	CHI	17	718	199	.510	10	.286	183	.799	26	119	130	42	13	591	34.8
89-90	CHI	16	674	219	.514	16	.320	133	.836	24	115	109	45	14	587	36.7
90-91	CHI	17	689	197	.524	10	.385	125	.845	18	108	142	40	23	529	31.1
91-92	CHI	22	920	290	.499	17	.386	162	.857	37	137	127	44	16	759	34.5
92-93	CHI	19	783	251	.475	28	.389	136	.805	32	128	114	39	17	666	35.1
Totals		111	4645	1411	.501	86	.352	942	.834	179	741	738	258	109	3850	34.7

NBA PLAYOFF RECORDS

- Highest career scoring average, 34.7.
- Most points in a playoff game, 63 vs. Boston on April 20, 1986.
- Highest scoring average in an NBA Finals series, 41.0 vs. Phoenix in 1993.
- Most points in an NBA Finals series, 246 vs. Phoenix in 1993.
- Most points in a three-game series, 135 vs. Miami in 1992.
- Most points in a five-game series, 226 vs. Cleveland in 1988.
- Most points in a half in an NBA Finals game, 35 vs. Portland on June 3, 1992.
- Tied for most 3-pointers made in an NBA Finals game, six vs. Portland on June 3, 1992.

NBA ALL-STAR GAME STATISTICS

		MIN	REB	AST	STL	3-PT	PTS
84-85	CHI	22	6	2	3	0	7
*85-86	CHI	—	—	—	—	—	—
86-87	CHI	28	0	4	2	0	11
87-88	CHI	29	8	3	4	0	40
88-89	CHI	33	2	3	5	0	28
89-90	CHI	29	5	2	5	1	17
90-91	CHI	36	5	5	2	0	26
91-92	CHI	31	1	5	2	0	18
92-93	CHI	36	4	5	4	1	30
Totals		244	31	29	27	2	177

* Selected but did not play because of injury.

NBA ALL-STAR GAME ACHIEVEMENTS

- All-Star Game MVP in 1987-88.
- Holds career record for highest career scoring average, 22.1.
- Won Slam Dunk Contest on All-Star Weekend, 1986-87 and 1987-88.

COLLEGE STATISTICS

		G	FGM	FGP	FTM	FTP	REB	PPG
81-82	UNC	34	191	.534	78	.722	149	13.5
82-83	UNC	36	282	.535	123	.737	197	20.0
83-84	UNC	31	247	.551	113	.779	163	19.6
Totals		101	720	.540	314	.748	509	17.7

COLLEGE ACHIEVEMENTS

- Won NCAA Championship with North Carolina, 1981-82.
- Named College Player of the Year by the *The Sporting News*, 1982-83 and 1983-84.
- Won gold medal as a member of the 1984 U.S. Olympic team.

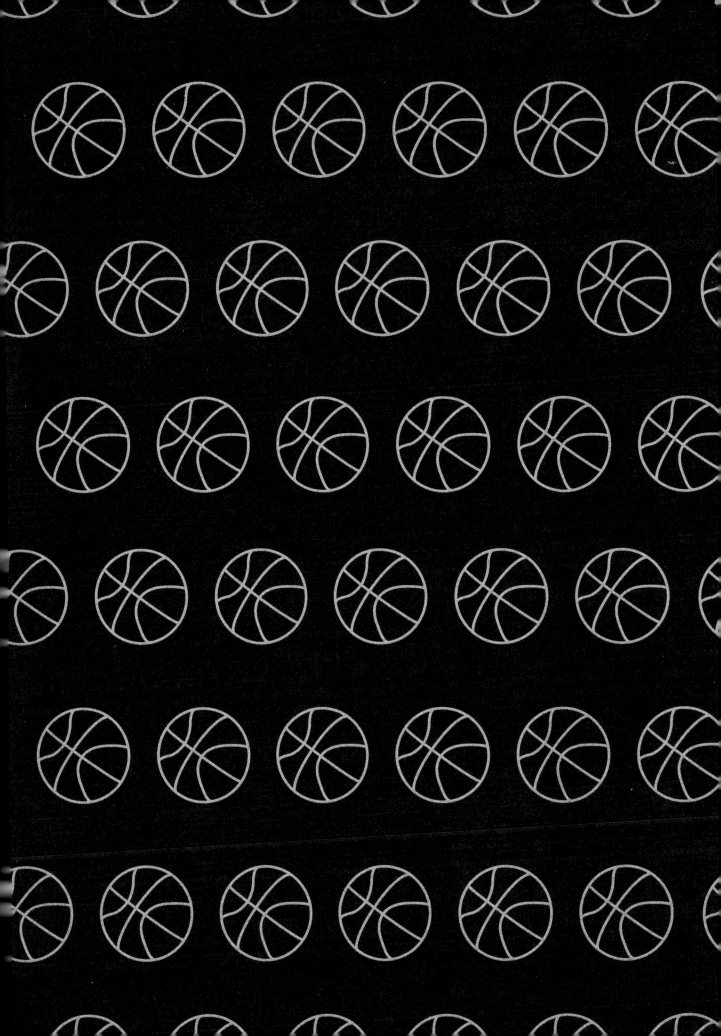